A Poetic Philosophy of Language

Bloomsbury Studies in Philosophy and Poetry

Series Editors: Rick Anthony Furtak, Colorado College, USA and James D. Reid, Metropolitan State University of Denver, USA

Editorial Board:

Daniel Brown, University of Southampton, UK
Kristen Case, University of Maine Farmington, USA
Hannah Vandegrift Eldridge, University of Wisconsin–Madison, USA
Cassandra Falke, University of Tromsø, Norway
Luke Fischer, University of Sydney, Australia
John Gibson, University of Louisville, USA
James Haile III, University of Rhode Island, USA
Kevin Hart, University of Virginia, USA
Eileen John, University of Warwick, UK
Troy Jollimore, California State University, USA
David Kleinberg-Levin, Northwestern University, USA
John Koethe, University of Wisconsin–Milwaukee, USA
John T. Lysaker, Emory University, USA
Karmen MacKendrick, Le Moyne College, USA
Rukmini Bhaya Nair, Indian Institute of Technology, India
Kamiyo Ogawa, Sophia University, Japan
Kaz Oishi, University of Tokyo, Japan
Yi-Ping Ong, Johns Hopkins University, USA
Anna Christina Soy Ribeiro, Texas Tech University, USA
Karen Simecek, University of Warwick, UK
Ruth Rebecca Tietjen, University of Copenhagen, Denmark
Íngrid Vendrell Ferran, Goethe University Frankfurt, Germany

Bloomsbury Studies in Philosophy and Poetry explores ancient, modern, and contemporary texts in ways that are sensitive to philosophical themes and problems that can be fruitfully addressed through poetic modes of writing, and focused on questions of style, the relations between form and content, and the conduciveness of literary modes of expression to philosophical inquiry. With a keen interest in the intertwining of poetry and philosophy in all forms, the series will cover the philosophical register of poetry, the poetics of philosophical writing, and the literary strategies of philosophers.

The series provides a home for work on figures across geographical landscapes, with contributions that employ a wide range of methods across academic disciplines, and without regard for divisions within philosophy, between analytic and continental, for example, that have outworn their usefulness. Featuring single-authored works and edited collections, curated by an international editorial board, the series aims to redefine how we read and discuss philosophy and poetry today.

Forthcoming Titles:

Philosophical Fragments and the Poetry of Thinking, by Luke Fischer
A Philosophy of Lyric Voice, by Karen Simecek
Skepticism and Impersonality in Modern Poetry, by Joshua Adams
A Black Poetics of the Everyday, by James Haile III

A Poetic Philosophy of Language

Nietzsche and Wittgenstein's Expressivism

Philip Mills

BLOOMSBURY ACADEMIC
LONDON · NEW YORK · OXFORD · NEW DELHI · SYDNEY

BLOOMSBURY ACADEMIC
Bloomsbury Publishing Plc
50 Bedford Square, London, WC1B 3DP, UK
1385 Broadway, New York, NY 10018, USA
29 Earlsfort Terrace, Dublin 2, Ireland

BLOOMSBURY, BLOOMSBURY ACADEMIC and the Diana logo are trademarks
of Bloomsbury Publishing Plc

First published in Great Britain 2022
This paperback edition published 2024

Copyright © Philip Mills, 2022

Philip Mills has asserted his right under the Copyright, Designs and Patents Act, 1988,
to be identified as Author of this work.

For legal purposes the Acknowledgements on p. vi constitute an extension
of this copyright page.

In the Current Six Thresholds (1929), Paul Klee.
Oil and tempera on canvas. (© GRANGER - Historical Picture Archive / Alamy)

All rights reserved. No part of this publication may be reproduced or transmitted in any
form or by any means, electronic or mechanical, including photocopying, recording, or
any information storage or retrieval system, without prior permission in writing from the
publishers.

Bloomsbury Publishing Plc does not have any control over, or responsibility for, any
third-party websites referred to or in this book. All internet addresses given in this
book were correct at the time of going to press. The author and publisher regret any
inconvenience caused if addresses have changed or sites have ceased to exist, but
can accept no responsibility for any such changes.

A catalogue record for this book is available from the British Library.

A catalog record for this book is available from the Library of Congress.

ISBN: HB: 978-1-3503-0008-8
PB: 978-1-3503-0014-9
ePDF: 978-1-3503-0011-8
eBook: 978-1-3503-0012-5

Series: Bloomsbury Studies in Philosophy and Poetry

Typeset by Deanta Global Publishing Services, Chennai, India

To find out more about our authors and books visit www.bloomsbury.com and
sign up for our newsletters.

Contents

Acknowledgements	vi
List of abbreviations	vii
A tale of two divides: Towards a philosophy of poetry	1
1 Language, representation and metaphysics	9
2 German philosophy of language as *Romantic Expressivism*	29
3 *Pragmatic Expressivism*: Brandom, Price, Blackburn	51
4 From Wittgenstein to Nietzsche and back	73
5 Poetry after Nietzsche and Wittgenstein	95
6 Towards a perspectival poetics	115
Conclusion: A poetic philosophy of language	137
Notes	145
Bibliography	158
Index	167

Acknowledgements

This book originates in my PhD thesis and would not exist without the help of all those who accompanied me during this process. I thank them all warmly. Andrew Bowie, my supervisor, for his always supportive and insightful criticism, as well as John Sellars and Henry Sommers-Hall from Royal Holloway. My examiners, Eileen John and Nicholas Davey, for turning the examination into a lively and open philosophical discussion. Stefan Majetschak for welcoming me as a visiting student at the University of Kassel. Herman Siemens and the participants at the Nietzsche Seminar in Leiden for inviting me to present some of my work. Isabelle Wienand for introducing me to Nietzsche and for her constant support ever since. All the people with whom I have discussed at conferences for raising many questions and broadening the scope of my research. The reviewers for pointing out useful suggestions and the editors at Bloomsbury for their efficient work. Finally, my mother Roseline Mills, for all these years she has had to endure reading philosophy because of me.

Abbreviations

Nietzsche

BGE	*Beyond Good and Evil*
BT	*The Birth of Tragedy*
D	*Daybreak*
DD	*Dionysus Dithyrambs*
GM	*On the Genealogy of Morals*
GS	*The Gay Science*
HH	*Human, All Too Human*
TI	*Twilight of the Idols*
TL	*On Truth and Lie in a Nonmoral Sense*
TSZ	*Thus Spoke Zarathustra*
WS	*The Wanderer and his Shadow*

Wittgenstein

BB	*The Blue and Brown Books*
CV	*Culture and Value*
LA	*Lectures on Aesthetics*

PG	*Philosophical Grammar*
PI	*Philosophical Investigations*
PPF	*Philosophy of Psychology – A Fragment* (former second part of the *Philosophical Investigations*)
RFM	*Remarks on the Foundations of Mathematics*
RPP	*Remarks on the Philosophy of Psychology, Volume 1*
T	*Tractatus Logico-Philosophicus*
Z	*Zettel*

I refer to Nietzsche's works by indicating the book title and the aphorism number, as well as the *Kritische Studienausgabe* (KSA) volume and page number. When referring to the notebooks, I indicate the KSA volume number and the note number. I refer to Wittgenstein's works by indicating the book title and aphorism, page or proposition number (or date in the case of the notebooks).

A tale of two divides

Towards a philosophy of poetry

> *Then let this be our defense – now that we've returned to the topic of poetry – that, in view of its nature, we had reason to banish it from the city earlier, for our argument compelled us to do so. But in case we are charged with a certain harshness and lack of sophistication, let's also tell poetry that there is an ancient quarrel between it and philosophy.*
>
> (Plato 1997, 1211, The Republic, 607a-b)

By siding with philosophy *against* poetry, Plato has turned poetry into a philosophical *problem*. Not only a problem to which philosophy has to attend, that is, an area that philosophical rationality needs to conceptualize, but also a problem that comes haunting philosophy by underlying its limits. The 'ancient quarrel between philosophy and poetry' becomes a quarrel about the legitimacy of discourse: Who of the poet or the philosopher is entitled to truth? Although the notions of philosophy and of poetry have evolved through time, Plato's setting of poetry as philosophy's 'other' seems to maintain an effectiveness throughout history, and its latest instantiation can be found in the so-called analytic–continental divide. In a very schematic way, analytic philosophy pursues Plato's ideal of removing poetry from the philosophical realm whereas continental philosophy embraces poetry as a means to knowledge. While we will see that this picture is far too schematic, the rejection of poetry has affected the field of analytic aesthetics as poetry remains, according to John Gibson's introduction to *The Philosophy of Poetry*, 'the last great unexplored frontier in contemporary aesthetics' (Gibson 2015, 1).

One of the concerns with this picture is that it relies on a divide which is itself already problematic. Indeed, when one takes a closer look, neither analytic nor continental philosophy seems to be a united and well-defined front. This is not to say that the divide has had no effect in the philosophical world (to the contrary as it shaped the twentieth-century philosophical landscape), but rather that these effects are produced less by an ontological difference than by a general misunderstanding of what philosophers on both sides try to do. For instance, in his assessment of analytic philosophy, Hans-Johann Glock notes twice that some aspects of analytic philosophy are closer to Nietzsche than one might initially think, thus weakening the sharp distinction the term 'divide' seems to suggest.[1] And even though the influence of this 'divide' is still quite strong for many philosophers, philosophy departments and philosophy journals, there is a continuity both historical and conceptual that unites both sides.

If, following Glock, analytic philosophy proves rather difficult to define as a united group of thinkers and appears much more to be a family resemblance concept in which some philosophers (e.g. Wittgenstein, Russell and Frege) are more influent than others (e.g. Hegel, Nietzsche and Heidegger), defining continental philosophy raises as many difficulties. As Simon Critchley argues, the distinction between analytic and continental philosophy 'is essentially a *professional self-description*, that is a way that departments of philosophy seek to organize their curricula and course offerings as well as signalling their broad intellectual allegiances' (Critchley 1997, 348, emphasis in original). These self-descriptions however hide, Critchley argues, broader cultural oppositions which suggest two conflictual understandings and definitions of philosophy. A wide range of oppositions can be established, and the most common ones include logicism versus anti-logicism, scientism versus anti-scientism, problems versus proper names and ahistorical versus historical. However, even though these broad strokes somehow paint a picture of the opposition between analytic and continental philosophy, they do not precisely outline what each is. Continental philosophy contains so many different schools of thought that it might be argued that the name 'continental' only unites them in a negative way, that is, as everything that is not analytic philosophy. When departments of philosophy with an analytic perspective categorize and subdivide philosophy into subjects such as metaphysics, epistemology and philosophy of mind, continental philosophy becomes such a category in which what does not enter other subdivisions can be placed.

In his study of the encounters between analytic and continental philosophy, Andrea Vrahimis also argues that the reason for the divide is to be found in 'extra-philosophical factors' rather than philosophical ones:

> In all of these encounters, it is not some irreconcilable clash between philosophical movements which is to be found; rather, extra-philosophical factors cause such misinterpretations. [. . .] This series of mistakes and omissions are caused by a drive towards picturing twentieth century philosophy as split in two, and have been instrumental in painting the haunting image of such a split. (Vrahimis 2013, 182)

Behind the twentieth-century depiction of philosophy as divided into two distinct traditions in conflict with one another lies a series of extra-philosophical misunderstandings. When one takes a closer look at the philosophers themselves, the divide becomes much thinner and both sides share much more than the word 'divide' suggests. More and more work is being done in connecting analytic and continental philosophers and some philosophers such as Richard Rorty and Stanley Cavell occupy a rather uncomfortable middle ground as they often look too analytic for continental philosophers and too continental for analytic ones.[2]

If analytic and continental turn out to be empty categories, as Glock, Critchley and Vrahimis consider, what has been called a divide can therefore not be seen as an obstacle to connecting philosophers from both sides. On the contrary, we will see that such dialogues open new possibilities for philosophy. In this framework, Nietzsche and Wittgenstein do not appear as radically opposed anymore, but as sharing some concerns regarding metaphysics and language, which offer key insights to elaborate a philosophy of poetry.

It might be objected that Nietzsche and Wittgenstein are not the most representative continental and analytic philosophers and that connecting them would therefore miss the target of overcoming the divide. However, as Cavell argues concerning Kierkegaard and Wittgenstein: 'while [they] may be untypical representatives of the philosophies for which I am making them stand, they are hardly peripheral to them. Any general comparison which could not accommodate these figures would also, if differently, risk irrelevance' (Cavell 1964, 946–7). Their belonging to the traditional picture of continental and analytic philosophy is further attested by their rejection from the opposite side: Carnap for instance considers Nietzsche as a poet more than a philosopher and Deleuze considers Wittgenstein as 'an assassin of philosophy' (Ayer 1959, 80; Deleuze and Parnet 1996, 'W comme Wittgenstein'). Wittgenstein's shift in style and concerns between his early and later works, however, makes the picture more complex, and his position within the history of philosophy is not so easy to pin down. If the *Tractatus* is considered as playing a foundational role in analytic philosophy, things become less clear with his later works. To the question 'Is Wittgenstein an analytic philosopher?' Anat Biletzki for instance answers: 'Yes, the early Wittgenstein was an analytic philosopher; no, the later was not' (Biletzki and Matar 2012, 197). But if one were to ask 'Is Wittgenstein a continental philosopher?' very few, I guess, would answer yes, disregarding early or late, and Deleuze's criticism of Wittgenstein suggests he would not want to be associated with him. However, as Glock argues, looking at the history of philosophy makes Wittgenstein's position easier to locate:

> when we look at the historical criterion, Wittgenstein's membership in the analytic tradition becomes clear. He was mainly influenced by analytic philosophers (Frege, Russell, Moore), and he in turn mainly influenced analytic philosophers (Russell, Moore, logical positivism, conceptual analysis). This is not to deny that he was also influenced by (Schopenhauer, James, Spengler) and influenced (hermeneutics, postmodernism) non-analytic philosophers. (Glock 2008, 226–7)

If analytic philosophy is a family resemblance concept, Wittgenstein belongs more to the analytic family than the continental one. Similarly, Nietzsche's influence on many twentieth-century continental philosophers (Heidegger, Deleuze and Derrida) makes him a central figure in continental philosophy.

One of the central concerns that Nietzsche and Wittgenstein share is the idea that philosophy *qua* metaphysics is an ill-founded enterprise. At the end of metaphysics, like many twentieth-century philosophers, they operate what has been called a 'linguistic turn' by considering that philosophical problems are rooted in language. However, while many philosophers operate such a shift, they do not agree on how language must be construed. Looking at two famous oppositions in the history of the analytic–continental divide – Carnap versus Heidegger and Searle versus Derrida – shows that a central point of disagreement concerns the place of poetry within a theory of language. Some philosophers, mostly continental, consider poetic language to be the essence of language, whereas others, mostly analytic, consider logic as the core matter and therefore exclude poetry. As we will see, this opposition reflects a broader opposition between a representational conception of language and an expressive one. Each view has its own problems: a representational conception of language fails to account for poetic uses and an expressive conception of language seems to open the door to a radical relativism in which nothing is fixed. While both Nietzsche and Wittgenstein share many concerns with the expressivist tradition, they manage to escape the charge of relativism by turning to a form of pragmatism.

By rooting itself in an investigation of language, a philosophy of poetry becomes not only a problem for poets and poetry theorists but also for philosophers of language, as French linguist Henri Meschonnic suggests that poetry is a challenge to thinking language:

> Poetry remains a challenge to thinking about language. It is a challenge because it requires revealing a conflict that philosophy has hidden in the same way it has hidden its lack of thinking about language. There is a need to better understand the relations between poetry and thinking, which leads to a poetics of philosophy.[3] (Meschonnic 2001, 265)

He further argues that philosophy has traditionally attempted to avoid this challenge, to divert attention from it, to 'exclude it from consideration' to borrow Austin's words (Austin 1975, 22). Taking poetry seriously from a philosophical point of view therefore entails that language cannot be construed solely in terms of representation and that truth is no longer a matter of correspondence between a statement and a fact. Truth cannot be taken in a metaphysical way, that is, as an eternal, absolute and context-independent truth, and this rejection of metaphysical truth breaks down the edifice Plato and many philosophers after him have built. In their song 'The Truth', poet-rapper Kae Tempest brings these elements together in a poetic way and stages the relativeness of truth. The song begins with the line 'It's all relative, right?' and this brings to a concise and efficient summary of Nietzsche's perspectivism: 'Is there a truth that exists / Outside of perception? / This is the question. / It's true if you believe it. / The world is the world / But it's all how you see it' (Tempest 2014). If truths cannot be considered as eternal and absolute, they must be relative to something, and Tempest suggests they are relative to perception. As we will see, Nietzsche's focus on perspective suggests a similar line of thought which modifies the hierarchies in philosophy: it does not only invert the rationalist move of considering reason over the senses (and therefore over perception) but also places aesthetics – in the etymological sense of *aisthēsis*, sensation or perception – at the centre of philosophical concerns over metaphysics. This idea of aesthetics goes back to the original use of the word by Alexander Baumgarten who considers it as the science of sensations (in contrast to reason). As Tempest suggests, the last and only meaningful metaphysical statement is a tautology: 'The world is the world.' This notion of tautology reminds us of Wittgenstein's *Tractatus* in which true statements are tautological and metaphysical statements meaningless. The important aspect in Tempest's song, however, is what comes after the metaphysical statement: 'but it's all how you see it'. This suggests a replacement of metaphysics by aesthetics: insofar as the only meaningful metaphysical statement is a tautology which says nothing about the world, the focus must shift from the 'objective' world to the way of seeing it. What Tempest suggests with this shift from metaphysics to aesthetics is, I argue, precisely the move Nietzsche makes in advocating for his perspectivism. Another important element is that the question of truth is translated in terms of beliefs: 'It's true if you believe it.' The question is no longer: 'what is true?' but 'what do you believe in?' Following Nietzsche's thought, this shift can be understood as moving from the question of truth to that of the value of truth. More precisely, Nietzsche questions the value of our usual conception of truth as correspondence between a statement and a fact. This conception is not the only way of understanding truth, and Nietzsche suggests that it might not always be the best way. What is in question is therefore not truth itself, or to that extent knowledge, reason, etc., but the value we give them, the belief we put into them.

This book is structured in six chapters moving from philosophy of language to philosophy of poetry. Chapter 1 criticizes traditional philosophy of language as relying on representationalism. In such a conception of language, meaning is grounded in reference – language represents a pre-existing world – and truth is a matter of correspondence. The problem of representationalism as Nietzsche and Wittgenstein point out is its strong metaphysical dimension: language is considered to reach the essence of the world, what Nietzsche calls a metaphysical true world. The focus on representation is also problematic for poetic uses of language that seem to escape the regime of reference and correspondence, that is, the regime of metaphysics. Against this metaphysical enterprise, Nietzsche and Wittgenstein belong to a pragmatic tradition in which the value of language lies in its use.

In Chapter 2, this pragmatic shift forces Nietzsche and Wittgenstein to elaborate an alternative conception of language that inherits from the expressive tradition of eighteenth- and nineteenth-century German philosophy.

According to Charles Taylor, the 'HHH view of meaning' (Herder, Humboldt, Heidegger) and the early German Romantics all work towards an alternative conception of language in which expression is key (Taylor 1985, 269). What can be called a *Romantic Expressivism* builds an alternative conception of truth as disclosure: the truth of a statement reveals something of the world. However, the idea of truth as disclosure retains a metaphysical dimension in the sense that it suggests that there is something hidden like a metaphysical true world to disclose, and that poetry is the key to access this hidden world. While Nietzsche clearly belongs to this tradition as he plays a pivotal role between the Romantics and Heidegger, Wittgenstein also inherits from this tradition, although more indirectly, notably through the influence of Fritz Mauthner and a broader 1900 Viennese *Zeitgeist* (Janik and Toulmin 1996).

Chapter 3 compares Taylor's expressive philosophy of language to contemporary expressivism, as found in the works of Robert Brandom, Huw Price and Simon Blackburn among others. In contrast to *Romantic Expressivism*, their view can be called a *Pragmatic Expressivism*. Pragmatism is understood here in a broad sense that includes Wittgenstein and even the early Heidegger, and, in the breadth of this scope, there can be some space for Nietzsche as well. One of the problems of *Pragmatic Expressivism* is that it pushes poetry out of the picture again. While *Romantic Expressivism* gives too much importance to poetry in its conception of language, *Pragmatic Expressivism* gives too little. This is where Nietzsche and Wittgenstein offer a more nuanced and balanced position.

Chapter 4 operates as the turning point in moving from philosophy of language to philosophy of poetry by considering Nietzsche's and Wittgenstein's views on language as lying at the intersection between *Romantic Expressivism* and *Pragmatic Expressivism*. They elaborate what could be called a *Poetic Expressivism* that leaves space open for poetry to occupy but does not fall in the extreme of considering poetry as the most important linguistic practice. However, in setting various linguistic practices as equal, Nietzsche and Wittgenstein seem to open a door to a form of 'anything goes' relativism. To escape this form of relativism, Nietzsche's notion of perspectivism is instrumental as a middle ground between the subjectivism of *Romantic Expressivism* and the rationalism of *Pragmatic Expressivism*.

Chapter 5 focuses specifically on poetry and shows that the *Poetic Expressivism* built on Nietzsche and Wittgenstein offers a way of approaching poetry from the perspective of philosophy of language. Against the idea that philosophy of language and poetry are obstacles to one another, a philosophy of poetry offers a poetic philosophy of language (rather than a philosophy of poetic language). Nietzsche and Wittgenstein move away from an essentialist definition of poetry to a wider family resemblance concept of poetics (which could therefore be applied to art forms other than poetry), and this occurs in the specific use of language that one finds in poetry. Building on Wittgenstein's 'seeing-as', poetry requires a certain form of 'reading-as'.

Following the conception of 'reading-as', Chapter 6 focuses on Nietzsche's perspectivism, more specifically his *aesthetic perspectivism*. Poetry offers new perspectives and brings the readers to experience these new perspectives. The difference between ordinary and poetic language is not one of kind (ontological, semantic or syntactic) but one of perspective and interpretation (pragmatic). Poetry, and other art forms, by forcing us to 'noticing aspects', ask that we look with a perspective that will highlight features of the world we might have otherwise overlooked. Nietzsche's perspectivism moves from *representationalism* to *expressivism*, and this move leads him to elaborate a poetic world view, a *perspectival poetics*, that leads him to account for the poetics of philosophy.

1

Language, representation and metaphysics

Well, Socrates, I've often talked with Cratylus – and with lots of other people, for that matter – and no one is able to persuade me that the correctness of names is determined by anything besides convention and agreement. I believe that any name you give a thing is its correct name. If you change its name and give it another, the new one is as correct as the old. For example, when we give names to our domestic slaves, the new ones are as correct as the old. No name belongs to a particular thing by nature, but only because of the rules and usage of those who establish the usage and call it by that name. However, if I'm wrong about this, I'm ready to listen not just to Cratylus but to anyone, and to learn from him too.

(Plato 1997, *Cratylus* 384c-d)

Plato's *Cratylus* opposes two conceptions of meaning: while Cratylus defends the idea that meaning is determined by the nature of the thing (or a divine instance), Hermogenes considers that meaning is determined only by convention. In terms of contemporary developments in philosophy of language, this opposition suggests two ways in which to consider the relation between word and world: to consider that names are determined by the nature of things places the emphasis on *reference* in determining meaning (semantics) whereas to focus on convention and agreement emphasizes the idea of meaning as *use* (pragmatics). Throughout the history of philosophy of language, and although some attempts have been made to combine them, semantics has often been given precedence over pragmatics. Wittgenstein's philosophy is interesting in this respect that his shift from the *Tractatus* to the later works can be interpreted as a move from one tradition to the other.

Deciding between semantics and pragmatics is an important philosophical question because the conception of meaning they respectively defend calls for a specific conception of truth. The basic conception of truth in the referential framework of semantics is that of *correspondence*: a statement is true if it corresponds to a fact. As Patricia Hanna and Bernard Harrison argue, such a theory relies on 'the existence of semantically mediated correlations between the members of some class of linguistic entities possessing assertoric force (in some versions of the Correspondence Theory propositions, in others sentences, or bodies of sentences), and the members of some class of extralinguistic entities: "states of affairs," or "facts," or bodies of truth-conditions, or of assertion-warranting circumstances' (Hanna and Harrison 2004). The theory of truth as correspondence therefore relies on a representational relation between language and the world: there is the world on one side and language represents it like a mirror. The importance of representation in such a theory of meaning and truth has led contemporary philosophers to coin the term *representationalism* to describe such a conception. Huw Price argues that there are two main elements to it:

> The view I'm challenging can be thought of as a loosely articulated combination of two fundamental assumptions about language and thought. The first assumption (call it the *content assumption*) is that language is a medium for encoding and passing around sentence-sized packets of factual information – the *contents* of beliefs and assertions. The second assumption (the *correspondence assumption*) is that these packets of information are all 'about' some aspect of the external world, in much the same way. (Price 2013, 40)

The two assumptions of representationalism are content and correspondence. As we have seen, the idea of correspondence suggests that language somehow mirrors the world, while the idea of content suggests that language is a game of transmitting information about the world (facts). These two assumptions are related to the idea that the truth of an information is determined by its relation to a fact in the world. Alongside other contemporary expressivists, Price rejects the notion of representationalism as it has, according him, outlived its usefulness. It has become too problematic, and he suggests replacing representation with a more pragmatic conception of language. Indeed, while representationalism fits some of our uses of language, there are some limits to it, which Wittgenstein outlines in his critique of Augustine's ostensive conception of language in the opening sections of PI. Furthermore, a field of language in which such a representational or ostensive conception of language fails is poetic and literary uses of language. As Wittgenstein suggests in Z: 'Do not forget that a poem, even though it is composed in the language of information, is not used in the language-game of giving information' (Z 160). The ideas of content and correspondence that are central to representationalism are challenged by such poetic uses because they fail to account for what is at play in such uses.

The aim of this chapter is to show that both Nietzsche and Wittgenstein reject representationalism because of its metaphysical dimension, and that this rejection opens a space for poetry within philosophy of language that we will explore in further chapters. The first part discusses Wittgenstein's idea that 'a picture held us captive' and shows that one of the problems of philosophy is its reliance on representationalism. The second part discusses Nietzsche's critique of metaphysics and establishes a parallel between Wittgenstein's picture and the idea of the 'true world' that Nietzsche criticizes in the chapter of TI 'How the true world finally became a fable'. The third part explores how we can escape representationalism by focusing on the pragmatic interpretation of Nietzsche and Wittgenstein given by Richard Rorty. This chapter sets the conceptual grounds for the exploration in Chapter 2 of a certain expressive tradition in eighteenth- and nineteenth-century German philosophy of language to which Nietzsche and Wittgenstein in some ways both belong and for the investigation in Chapter 3 of its relation to contemporary expressivism as defended by Robert Brandom, Huw Price and Simon Blackburn. By showing that Nietzsche and Wittgenstein belong to a same tradition which influences contemporary developments in analytic philosophy, these chapters aim to show that the so-called analytic–continental divide is in fact much thinner than it seems and that there are many ways of overcoming it.

1 'A picture held us captive': The representational conception of language

According to Wittgenstein, philosophy has been held captive by a certain picture, the picture of representationalism. Wittgenstein introduces this idea in a series of remarks in PI:

114. *Tractatus Logico-Philosophicus* (4.5): 'The general form of propositions is: This is how things are.' – This is the kind of proposition one repeats to oneself countless times. One thinks that one is tracing nature over and over again, and one is merely tracing round the frame through which we look at it.

115. A picture held us captive. And we couldn't get outside of it, for it lay in our language, and language seemed only to repeat it to us inexorably.

116. When philosophers use a word – 'knowledge,' 'being,' 'object,' 'I,' 'proposition/sentence,' 'name' – and try to grasp the *essence* of the thing, one must always ask oneself: is the word ever actually used in this way in the language in which it is at home? –

What *we* do is to bring words back from their metaphysical to their everyday use.

In his later works, Wittgenstein considers that the *Tractatus* was misguided in thinking that it could reach the essence of language insofar as it was still a metaphysical move. The proposition is only building the frame through which the world is seen and is not connected to the essence of the world. This is the picture of representationalism: when we use language, we are saying something about the world that can be verified in terms of correspondence. The problem with this picture is that it moves from a linguistic question to a metaphysical one. Philosophers are captive of this picture because it lies in their language, because they are thinking that with language they are connected to the essence of the world. This picture is especially salient when philosophers use certain words to which they attribute special significance. However, these words remain unproblematic in our everyday use of language. To solve philosophical problems is to bring language back home.

In moving away from the *Tractatus*, Wittgenstein operates a shift from semantics to pragmatics or, to use Rorty's terminology in *The Linguistic Turn*, from ideal language philosophy to Ordinary Language Philosophy.[1] In the *Tractatus*, Wittgenstein follows the tradition of ideal language philosophy in line with Gottlob Frege and Bertrand Russell. The Frege-Russell-*Tractatus* line marks the birth of analytic philosophy, which Michael Dummett places in Frege's 1884 *Grundlagen der Arithmetik*[2] and Hans-Johann Glock in Frege's development of formal logic in his *Begriffschtrift*.[3] This focus on logic leads Frege to distinguish between the 'logical content' of signs and their 'colouring', dismissing the latter as irrelevant to meaning. As Dummett argues: 'The sense is that part of the meaning of an expression which is relevant to the determination of the truth-value of a sentence in which the expression may occur; the colouring is that part of its meaning which is not (for instance, that which distinguishes "chap" from "guy" and from "man")' (Dummett 1978, 93). From the outset, this distinction seems therefore to disdain poetic and literary uses of language which rely on such 'colouring'. However, Frege makes another and more fundamental distinction between *sense (Sinn)* and *reference (Bedeutung)* in 'On *Sinn* and *Bedeutung*'. His main idea is that 'the regular connection between a sign, its sense and its *Bedeutung* is of such a kind that to the sign there corresponds a definite sense and to that in turn a definite *Bedeutung*, while to a given *Bedeutung* (an object) there does not belong only a single sign. The same sense has different expressions in different languages or even in the same language' (Frege 1997, 153). This distinction is required to account either for expressions without reference or different expressions having the same reference such as Frege's example of the 'morning star' and the 'evening star' which both refer to Venus. Frege considers that there is an important difference between *Sinn* and *Bedeutung* in their relation to truth. As Glock summarizes: 'their meaning (*Bedeutung*), which is the object they refer to, and their sense (*Sinn*), the "mode of presentation" of that referent. [. . .] The meaning of a sentence is its truth-value; its sense is the "thought" it expresses' (Glock 2008, 29). In an expression, the bearer of the truth-value is thus the *Bedeutung*, and this is why Frege requires such a notion: 'But now why do we want every proper name to have not only a sense, but also a *Bedeutung*? Why is the thought not enough for us? Because, and to the extent that, we are concerned with its truth-value. This is not always the case' (Frege 1997, 157). In attributing truth-value to *Bedeutung*, Frege prevents any expressions without referent, that is, any fictional expression, to be either true or false, without making them meaningless. Indeed, one of the problems of too straightforward a conception of meaning as reference is that expressions without reference become meaningless, and literary statements cannot be said to be meaningless although they lack reference. However, Frege's theory allows poetic statements to have a *Sinn*; it prevents them from having any truth-value, and his rejection of 'colouring' outside the realm of meaning cuts away something crucial to poetic statements.

Following Frege, Russell tackles the problem of sentences without reference. A similar question thus arises, as Ayer quotes and comments on Russell: '"How can a non-entity be the subject of a proposition?" Russell does not think that any of these difficulties can be met by having recourse to Frege's well-known distinction between sense and reference' (Ayer 1971, 30). To solve the problem, Russell elaborates a theory of descriptions, which attempts to give an account of sentences without reference while remaining within a general conception of meaning based on reference. According to Russell's theory, meaning can be replaced by definite descriptions; words are not names in the sense of proper names which have a direct connection to the object or person, but as it were abbreviations for descriptions. As William Lycan summarizes, Russell takes Frege in the opposite way: 'Thus names do have what Frege thought of as "senses," that can differ despite sameness of referent, but Russell gives an analysis of these rather than taking them as primitive items of some abstract sort' (Lycan 2008, 35). Although meant to solve the problems of fictional referents, Russell's theory still struggles with sentences such as the famous: 'The present king of France is bald.' How can a sentence have a truth-value if the object does not exist? Is the sentence about the king of France true or false? It is not a meaningless sentence for it is very understandable, but from a referential perspective, it is problematic. As it has no truth-value, it cannot have a meaning. Both Frege's and Russell's theories attempt to solve problems that a conception of language encounters when meaning is based on reference, and such problems are the most visible when confronting such a theory to poetic or literary works. The literary aspects of language thus appear more as problems than insights to explore further and the early Wittgenstein shows equally little concern with literary uses of language in his *Tractatus*.

Wittgenstein's *Tractatus* relies on the same presuppositions, namely that philosophy ought to clarify language, that language represents the world and that sentences have meaning in relation to their truth-value. In the *Tractatus*, Wittgenstein is perhaps even more radical than Frege and Russell as he comes to consider only the propositions of science as being meaningful, although having nothing to do with philosophy: 'The correct method in philosophy would really be the following: to say nothing except what can be said, i.e. propositions of natural science – i.e. something that has nothing to do with philosophy – and then, whenever someone else wanted to say something metaphysical, to demonstrate to him that he had failed to give a meaning to certain signs in his propositions' (T, 6.53). Only the propositions of science can be said, all the rest must be kept silent because it cannot meaningfully be put into words: 'There are, indeed, things that cannot be put into words. They *make themselves manifest*. They are what is mystical' (T, 6.522) More precisely, what cannot be put into words are ethics and aesthetics. This rejection of ethics and aesthetics into the 'mystical' is a way of explicitly rejecting 'deviant' uses of language outside of the realm of the meaningful. To that extent, Wittgenstein makes explicit Frege's and Russell's rejection of poetic uses from the realm of philosophy of language.

These three conceptions of language are all captive of representationalism which leads them to consider poetic and literary uses of language as deviances, as problems. This idea that poetic uses are a problem for philosophy of language remains strongly shared among philosophers of language, as Lycan's *Introduction to Philosophy of Language* for instance places such uses in a part entitled 'The dark side' containing only one chapter on metaphors[4] (Lycan 2008, 173–90). Poetic, literary, metaphorical sentences therefore reveal a weakness of representationalism and hence of most philosophies of language. Frege denies any truth-value to such sentences, Russell elaborates a complex theory to distinguish these sentences from 'normal' sentences, and Wittgenstein rejects ethics and aesthetics as belonging to the 'mystical'. This failure in accounting for such uses of language, which can be rather common in everyday usage as the use of metaphor is not limited to poetic works, is a hint that representationalism might not be the best suited to understand how language works. They are conceptions of an 'ideal language', which, like its name indicates, might never be encountered in the actual world.

Wittgenstein's critique of the *Tractatus* in PI 114 reveals the shift he operates regarding this tradition. He moves away from the Frege-Russell-*Tractatus* line and towards what has been called Ordinary Language Philosophy. Philosophy is no longer the search for an ideal language but the description of ordinary uses of language:

> It is wrong to say that in philosophy we consider an ideal language as opposed to our ordinary one. For this makes it appear as though we thought we could improve on ordinary language. But ordinary language is all right. Whenever we make up 'ideal languages' it is not in order to replace our ordinary language by them; but just to remove some trouble caused in someone's mind by thinking that he has got hold of the exact use of a common word.

> That is also why our method is not merely to enumerate actual usages of words, but rather deliberately to invent new ones, some of them because of their absurd appearance. (*BB*, p. 28)

This remark from the *Blue Book* shows that there is an important creative dimension to Wittgenstein's ordinary language. While there is a conservative picture of language in Austin and most ordinary language philosophers, Wittgenstein suggests that invention plays a central role which opens a space for poetic uses of language, a space that Austin for instance rejects.[5] 'Ordinary language is all right,' there is no need to improve it, but we must investigate how we use it. And that means investigate how we could use it by inventing new uses. Wittgenstein already suggests something like this in the *Tractatus*: 'In fact, all the propositions of our everyday language, just as they stand, are in perfect logical order' (T 5.5563). But whereas the *Tractatus* emphasizes the logical order of language, the later works do not attempt to reduce language to logic.

2 Nietzsche, metaphysics and the seduction of language

We have seen that Wittgenstein's critique of representationalism is grounded in his critique of metaphysics and essentialism: the notions of reference and truth as correspondence mislead us into believing that language expresses the essence of things. This metaphysical move establishes what Nietzsche calls a 'true world' behind the apparent one: language would be the world of appearances behind which lies a metaphysical 'true world'. Nietzsche makes this distinction in the famous TI chapter 'How the true world finally became a fable'. In six steps, Nietzsche presents the history of metaphysics – 'the history of an error' – from Plato's setting up the philosopher's true world against the world of appearances to the abolition of the whole dualism between true and apparent worlds: 'The true world is gone: which world is left? The illusory one, perhaps? . . . But no! *we got rid of the illusory world along with the true one!*' (TI 'How the True World' / KSA 6.81, emphasis in original). This dualism between true and apparent worlds is a metaphysical error and even the 'longest error' which must be overcome. Anticipating some aspects of the twentieth-century linguistic turn, Nietzsche considers that such errors can be overcome by turning our attention to language.

Indeed, Nietzsche suggests in HH that language is the birthplace of metaphysics: 'The significance of language for the development of human culture lies in the fact that human beings used it to set up a world of their own beside the other one, a place they deemed solid enough that from there they could lift the rest of world from its hinges and make themselves its master' (HH 11 / KSA 2.30). This idea of mastering the world is not unrelated to Descartes's idea in the *Discourse* that science would make 'ourselves as it were masters and possessors of nature' (Descartes 2006, 51). Although science and language are related for Nietzsche, and especially in this paragraph from HH, he shifts his focus from science – and Descartes's concern with epistemology – to language, thus operating a 'linguistic turn'. It is with language that humankind sets up a so-called true world besides the apparent one. More precisely, as Nietzsche continues, it is the belief in concepts as '*aeternae veritates*' that leads to metaphysical fallacies: the main feature of metaphysics is to make human beings believe that when they talk about a concept, they are talking about the world, so that 'they really [believe] that in language they [have] knowledge of the world' (HH 11 / KSA 2.30). This is a critique of Plato's doctrine of ideas and the metaphysical conception of language according to which a word refers to a Platonic idea in a direct fashion.[6]

This critique of metaphysical uses of language relies more specifically on a critique of concepts and of the relation between word and world:

> The word and the concept are the most visible reason for why we believe in this isolation of groups of actions: with them, we are not simply *designating* things, we originally think that through them we are grasping the *essence* of things. So now, we are continuously misled by words and concepts to think of things as being more simple than they are, separated from one another, indivisible, each one existing in and for itself. A philosophical mythology lies concealed in *language*, which breaks forth again at every moment, however careful we may otherwise be. (WS 11 / KSA2.547)

Words and concepts lead to a metaphysical use of language, and Nietzsche's task is to reveal the whole 'philosophical mythology' underlying the use of language and especially that of the metaphysicians. His problem with language is that it is used not only to designate but also and above all to generalize and regroup things in categories. This idea is central to TL, in which he considers words and concepts to be the result of metaphorical transpositions: 'To begin with, a nerve stimulus is transferred into an image: first metaphor. The image, in turn, is imitated in a sound: second metaphor' (TL 1 / KSA 1.879). Once the perceptual metaphors become fixed (and thus lose their uniqueness), they die and become words which immediately become concepts: 'a word becomes a concept insofar as it simultaneously has to fit countless more or less similar cases' (TL 1 / KSA 1.879). What Nietzsche criticizes in concepts is their propensity towards generalization: many perceptual metaphors must fit under one concept – what Wittgenstein calls the 'craving for generality'.

One of the main problems Nietzsche has with definite concepts is that they equate unequal things: 'Every concept arises from the equating of unequal things' (TL 1 / KSA 1.880). Concepts are thus born from equating individual metaphors. In other words, concepts oppose metaphors like generality opposes particularity.[7] There is, however, a filiation between metaphors and concepts: 'the concept [. . .] is nevertheless merely the *residue of a metaphor*, and that illusion which is involved in the artistic transference of a nerve stimulus into images is, if not the mother, then the grandmother of every single concept' (TL 1 / KSA 1.882). How does this fixing happen? Mainly because we forget the metaphorical origin of all concepts:

> Only by forgetting this primitive world of metaphor can one live with any repose, security, and consistency: only by means of the petrification and coagulation of a mass of images which originally streamed from the primal faculty of human imagination like a fiery liquid, only in the invincible faith that *this* sun, *this* window, *this* table is a truth in itself, in short, only by forgetting that he himself is an artistically creating subject, does man live with any repose, security, and consistency. (TL 1 / KSA1.883)

This forgetting of the metaphorical origins of language is necessary for human beings to live because without this 'invincible faith', without this metaphysical belief in words, there could be no communication at all. The social and scientific edifice is built on the belief in such a conceptual relation between word and world. If there were only the original metaphors (from nerve stimuli to images) and no equating of unequal things, no transformation into words, communication would be impossible for there would be nothing common to talk about.[8] For Nietzsche, human beings must therefore abandon their artistically creative selves in order to live in community; they must abandon the original metaphors in favour of concepts, and this is perhaps why Nietzsche considers the human realization that this belief in language, this 'tremendous error,' happens 'luckily [. . .] too late for the development of reason, which rests upon that belief, to be reversed' (HH 11 / KSA 2.30).

In contrast, artists live as artistically creative subjects, and art is the only place where the 'drive to form metaphors', this 'fundamental human drive', is free. Here, Nietzsche attributes a creative force to art and poetry, thus giving a positive evaluation of poetry rather than considering it a deviance. Indeed, everyday life and its necessary stability imprison creativity; in everyday life, humans must forget their artistic ability to create new metaphors. But this forgetting also prevents humans from seeing new things, and discoveries are left for artists. In other words, 'the way men usually are, it takes a name to make something visible for them. – Those with originality have for the most part also assigned names' (GS 261 / KSA 3.517). Language does not only mirror the world, but takes part into shaping it. To see the world, or things in the world, one needs to possess the words to grasp them. To that extent, metaphors are not mere comparisons but open our ways of seeing the world. In the next chapters, we will explore this idea as a shift from *representationalism* to *expressivism*.

In BGE, Nietzsche pursues this idea of the 'common' character of language, broadening the view he held in TL:[9] 'Words are acoustic signs for concepts; concepts, however, are more or less precise figurative signs for frequently recurring and simultaneous sensations, for groups of sensations. Using the same words is not enough to ensure mutual understanding: we must also use the same words for the same category of inner experiences; ultimately, we must have the same experience in *common*' (BGE 268 / KSA 5.221). Nietzsche's insistence on the 'common' places the emphasis on the conventional dimension of language, thus siding with Hermogenes against Cratylus (and hence Socrates and Plato). In contrast to the artistically creative subjects, that is 'uncommon' or 'extraordinary' subjects, everyday people use language as it is established by convention and this affects the concepts of knowledge and truth.

In TL, Nietzsche already argues against the correspondence theory of truth:

This peace treaty brings in its wake something which appears to be the first step toward acquiring that puzzling truth drive: to wit, that which shall count as 'truth' from now on is established. That is to say, a uniformly

> valid and binding designation is invented for things, and this legislation
> of language likewise establishes the first laws of truth. For the contrast
> between truth and lie arises here for the first time. The liar is a person
> who uses the valid designations, the words, in order to make something
> which is unreal appear to be real. He says, for example, 'I am rich,' when
> the proper designation for his condition would be 'poor.' He misuses fixed
> conventions by means of arbitrary substitutions or even reversals of names.
> (TL 1 / KSA1.877)

If language and its rules are conventional, the difference between truth and lie is not a difference of fact but a difference of use, or a difference of value. The correspondence is not between a statement and a fact but between a statement and a convention. Liars use words in a way which does not conform to the rules established by the community – the dominant perspective – and are therefore excluded from it. An intelligent liar, however, uses and interprets the rules in order to make her claims seem true (this, to some extent, is the whole point of Plato's critique of the Sophists). In the passage quoted earlier, Nietzsche exposes the correspondence theory of truth: liars are those who say 'I am rich' when 'poor' would have been the right description. The notion of truth Nietzsche discusses here is thus entirely dependent on language and on the conventions or rules embedded in it. What is true is what conforms to the rules. A shift in language-game – and therefore a shift in rules – would lead to a revaluation of truth: something true in one game might be false in another and vice versa. Truth depends on what language-game is played and rules attribute values to things: true, false, beautiful, ugly, good, evil, etc. These values aren't absolute – hence Nietzsche's critique of absolute concepts and *'aeternae veritates'* – they are cultural. Nietzsche's critique of language is a critique of humankind's belief in a metaphysical language in which values are not relative but absolute.

This belief in a metaphysical conception of language, representationalism, is the result of philosophers being seduced by language. The metaphor of seduction is a recurrent feature in Nietzsche's works, and the preface to BGE compares truth to a woman whom philosophers attempt to charm.[10] Their failure in seducing this woman might indicate that it is they who are being charmed rather than the opposite. Uncovering the 'mythology' which underlies language, Nietzsche criticizes the idea of a divine origin of language. According to Rorty:

To drop the idea of language as representations, and to be thoroughly Wittgensteinian in our approach to language, would be to de-divinize the world. Only if we do that can we fully accept the argument I offered earlier – the argument that since truth is a property of sentences, since sentences are dependent for their existence upon vocabularies, and since vocabularies are made by human beings, so are truths. (Rorty 1989, 21)

To say with Nietzsche that 'God is dead' is to say that language is no longer a divine creation but a human practice. If language is a human creation, it has a history. Concepts do not fall down from 'cloud cuckoo land', to borrow Nietzsche's image in TL but have a human origin and are subject to development. To use a Derridean term, concepts can now be deconstructed and, most importantly, so can the concept of concept.[11]

The seduction which holds the philosophers captive – 'the picture that held us captive' – leads them to metaphysical errors. The problem is not language itself but the metaphysician's belief in it. Because they are seduced by it, metaphysicians do not realize that the language they believe in is 'magic' as Samuel Wheeler calls it or metaphysical in the sense that the words are taken as referring directly to objects in the world: they take words as naming the essence of things. For Nietzsche, language is a social practice established by convention and use rather than an eternal truth. Forgetting this, metaphysicians fall into the traps laid by language, and one of the greatest errors they make is to believe in and to use abstract concepts: 'But I shall repeat a hundred times over that the "immediate certainty," like "absolute knowledge" and the "thing in itself," contains a *contradiction in adjecto*: it's time people freed themselves from the seduction of words!' (BGE 16 / KSA 5.29). Nietzsche exhorts us to free ourselves from the charms of language. The 'thing-in-itself' and similar concepts are all linguistic creations and must not be taken as metaphysical categories. In order to reach knowledge, we must look into language and try unfolding all that is embedded in it. In the remaining of the aphorism, Nietzsche presents his critique of the philosophers' use of language aimed at Descartes's 'I think' and Schopenhauer's 'I will'. Nietzsche shows that by saying 'I think', Descartes presupposes that the notion of 'I' is something simple and that 'thinking' is somehow unified. According to Nietzsche, the 'I' cannot be construed in such simplistic terms: it is a complex notion which cannot be posited in the way Descartes does and 'thinking' includes many nuances which Descartes does not take into account. Metaphysical language abolishes most of the nuances which make the world we live in what it is. This critique (which is, through the reference to Descartes, a critique of how metaphysics rely on, without putting it into question, a 'magic' language) leads Nietzsche to question not only language itself but, as in most of the first section of BGE, the 'will to truth' and why truth should be privileged over untruth.

According to Nietzsche, we must escape the seduction of language and his invective to free ourselves from metaphysical conceptions embedded in language can remind us of Wittgenstein's aim to 'bring back words from their metaphysical use to their ordinary' (PI 116). But this is not the only connection to Wittgenstein. They both undertake a task of clarifying language: Nietzsche by revealing the metaphysical and axiological prejudices embedded in language and Wittgenstein by showing the meaninglessness of metaphysical propositions. However, philosophy must not change language, because it would fall back in the enterprise of ideal language philosophy, it must 'leave everything as it is' (PI 124). What it can do is to change the way we relate to such a language; we can try and free ourselves from the metaphysical trap of representationalism. One way of doing so is to shift from semantics to pragmatics.

3 Escaping representationalism: The task of pragmatism

Insofar as it relies on a metaphysical true world, Nietzsche and Wittgenstein both agree on rejecting representationalism. But without representationalism, the project of traditional semantics cannot hold. As mentioned earlier, the alternative to semantics is pragmatics, and the move away from representationalism can therefore be understood as a first step towards pragmatism. Indeed, Robert Brandom construes pragmatism as opposed to representationalism:

> Fundamental pragmatism is opposed to a *representationalist* order of explanation: one that begins with a notion of representational content, and appeals to that notion to make sense of what it is that knowing and acting subjects *do*. That is not to say that pragmatists in this sense can have no truck at all with the concept of *representation*. It is to say at most that talk of representation should come at the end of the story, not the beginning. (Brandom 2011, 11, underline in original)

The problem is not with representation per se but with the fact that we consider representation to be the beginning of the story. In philosophy of language, this privilege given to representation (and hence to semantics) has overshadowed many linguistic phenomena and has always retained a form of metaphysical dimension. Pragmatism, to the contrary, focuses on the linguistic practices themselves and moves away from this picture of language as a mirror, following Rorty's *Philosophy as the Mirror of Nature* (Rorty 2009). It inverts the order of explanation: rather than beginning with representation as justification for our actions, pragmatism begins with what Brandom calls 'what it is that knowing and acting subjects *do*'. Some of our doings have something to do with representation according to Brandom, but not all of them. Representation can therefore not be taken as the grounding principle to justify our linguistic practices. Shifting from a representationalist to a pragmatist order of explanation does not entail a rejection of representation but, using a Nietzschean vocabulary, a revaluation of the value of representation, of its role and place among our concepts.

While Wittgenstein's place in the pragmatist tradition is relatively secured, Nietzsche's relation to pragmatism is more complex. Pietro Gori argues that Nietzsche's perspectivism has affinities with pragmatism, especially in its rejection of the correspondence theory of truth. His aim is not 'to make a pragmatist out of Nietzsche, but only let him dialogue with a philosophical perspective that – as happened with Nietzsche himself – has been soon simplified and misinterpreted, so that nowadays it is difficult to deal with it properly' (Gori 2019, 4). The proximity that Nietzsche's thought entertains with pragmatism has brought him to be an influent figure for some contemporary pragmatists such as Rorty who connect him to the pragmatic tradition including Wittgenstein. Rorty's reading of Nietzsche establishes him as a pragmatic thinker opposed to representationalism: language is no longer thought to represent the world, but to constitute it. However, we should not understand this notion of constitution as establishing a causal relation between language and the world, as Rorty argues:

> The Nietzschean view I have been sketching is often described as the doctrine that everything is 'constituted' by language, or that everything is 'socially constructed,' or that everything is 'mind dependent'. But these descriptions are hopelessly misleading. Words like 'constitution' and 'construction' and 'dependence,' in the language games that are their original homes, refer to

causal relations. [...] Causal relations hold only within what Nietzsche called 'a certain calculable world of identical cases' – a world of identifiable objects. We can investigate causal relations once we have identified such objects, but there is no point in asking where the world that contains such objects comes from. (Rorty 2016, 15–16)

One of the problems in the way Nietzsche's view is thought of is the causality it suggests. Language is not the cause of the world as much as the world is not the cause of language (as in the representationalist idea of the mirror). Causal relations can be established only once the objects between which they occur have been set. However, in the world and language relation, it is impossible to set one and the other separately; the world and language are established simultaneously through a mutual shaping.

This idea goes in the direction of Romanticism – shifting from the 'mirror' to the 'lamp' conception of language following M. H. Abrams (Abrams 1977) – that Rorty defines as: 'the thesis that what is most important for human life is not what propositions we believe but what vocabulary we use' (Rorty 1981, 158). What Romanticism brings to the fore is the idea that the vocabulary we use is the most important thing to understand our relation to the world. However, this definition still contains a metaphysical dimension, and a further step is needed, namely from Romanticism to pragmatism:

> This was the step taken by Nietzsche and William James. Their contribution was to replace romanticism by pragmatism. Instead of saying that the discovery of vocabularies could bring hidden secrets to light, they said that new ways of speaking could help get us what we want. Instead of hinting that literature might succeed philosophy as discoverer of ultimate reality, they gave up the notion of truth as a correspondence to reality. (Rorty 1981, 165)

While Romanticism, as we will see in Chapter 2, has a metaphysical dimension in the idea that language (or literature), the right vocabulary as it were, can reveal something hidden, what has been coined as the idea of truth as disclosure, pragmatism remains at the level of practices without searching for something hidden behind or underneath.

In this framework, representation is only one vocabulary among many others. In discussing Rorty's rejection of representation, Blackburn highlights not only the idea that there can be no world from nowhere, that is, that we are always standing in the world (we are always using a specific vocabulary in Rorty's words) and that we must take this into account, but also the idea that in supposing a privileged vocabulary the representationalist is making a metaphysical move that has no ground to justify it:

> Representing the world correctly then becomes representing the world in the way it demands to be talked about. Rorty often presents his realist opponent as supposing that there is 'one privileged discourse' or a preferred vocabulary: the vocabulary of the Book of Nature. The enemy is the idea that 'the final vocabulary of physics will somehow be Nature's own', or that there is a vocabulary that is 'somehow already out there in the world, waiting for us to discover it'. (Blackburn 2007, 153)

Coined in the vocabulary of perspectivism, the two arguments Blackburn highlights in Rorty are the following: (1) there can be no aperspectival seeing (we are always in a perspective) and (2) there is no privileged perspective (at least not metaphysically). The representationalist supposes that there is a preferred vocabulary, that of nature, and that nature therefore demands to be talked about in a specific way. But this idea opens the door to the metaphysical 'true world' that Nietzsche criticizes. Supposing that our discourse should meet the demands of nature is supposing that there is such a thing as an absolute nature that exists independently from our perspectives on it. But if this nature can never be experienced (because our experiences of nature are dependent on our perspectives), the representationalist appeal to an absolute nature is a metaphysical move. Following the representationalist, our discourse must meet the demands of something that, in a Kantian sense, we can never fully know because we can never reach the thing-in-itself. In other words, the pragmatist would ask: Why do you need a metaphysical true world when you can never experience it?

We have seen that both Nietzsche and Wittgenstein agree in rejecting this metaphysical 'true world' and shift their attention to our linguistic practices. In this pragmatic shift towards language, Rorty does not leave poetry aside. On the contrary as he considers poetry to be pointing philosophy towards a form of pluralism: 'To take the side of the poets in this quarrel is to say that there are many descriptions of the same things and events, and that there is no neutral standpoint from which to judge the superiority of one description over another. Philosophy stands in opposition to poetry just insofar as it insists that there is such a standpoint' (Rorty 2016, 20). Traditional philosophy (i.e. metaphysics) is opposed to poetry insofar as it suggests that there is a privileged perspective, a privileged vocabulary, most often, the vocabulary of nature. In contrast to the idea that language represents the world, we must think of it as creating the world in the etymological sense of poeticizing the world. This is what Rorty finds in Nietzsche: 'When Nietzsche urged us to "see science through the optic of art," he was suggesting that we should see new scientific theories not as representations of the real but as poetic achievements' (Rorty 2016, 18). And to a further extent, philosophy too can be seen through the optic of art as a poetic achievement, because language is essentially poetic in the etymological sense of *poiesis*. Richard Poirier, who connects pragmatism to poetry, suggests:

> According to this theory of entitlements, our language is full of essentially poetic associations, and anyone who uses it is therefore to some degree a poet. So that when I speak of 'poetry and pragmatism' I again mean not simply that some pragmatist philosophers have had an influence on poets; I mean that in their own uses of words they too are poets, just as the poets are also philosophers. (Poirier 1993, 103)

If language is full of poetic associations, that is, if poetic language is not separated from the ordinary, pragmatism, insofar as it focuses on ordinary linguistic practices, has a close relationship with poetry.[12]

One of the reasons for this proximity comes from the idea that pragmatism as poetry is concerned with change, as Poirier argues: 'If pragmatism works, then it works the way poetry does – be effecting a change of language, a change carried out entirely *within* language, and for the benefit of those destined to inherit the language' (Poirier 1993, 132). At the heart of philosophy is therefore no longer the idea of reaching the perfect representation, of getting it right, but the idea of creating and transforming ourselves following Nietzsche and Rorty:

> As I said in my first lecture, Nietzsche gave a different answer than Plato's to the question about what makes human beings special. He said it was our ability to transform ourselves into something new, rather than our ability to know what we ourselves really are or what the universe is really like. He mocked Plato's appearance-reality distinction, a distinction that most analytic philosophers still take for granted. (Rorty 2016, 31)

Against Plato's appearance–reality distinction, Nietzsche argues that we must create ourselves and transform ourselves. Hence, we are no longer passive subjects but active agents creating ourselves and the world anew.[13] We are not only rational creatures able to think how the world is but imaginative creatures able to create new games: 'Rationality is a matter of making allowed moves within language-games. Imagination creates the games that reason proceeds to play' (Rorty 2016, 15). This focus on imagination brings Romanticism back into the picture. In his move from Romanticism to pragmatism, Nietzsche does not abandon the Romantic ideal of imagination. There is a Romantic dimension to Nietzsche's pragmatism that makes it different from classical American pragmatism.

Moreover, Rorty argues, Romanticism and pragmatism are not so far away from one another:

> Pragmatism and romanticism will seem opposed to one another if we think of the one as urging us to adopt practicality as a criterion and the other telling us that only imagination matters. One can make pragmatism look absurd by ascribing it as the proposal that we use some version of the utilitarian calculus as a criterion for theory choice or for resolving moral dilemmas. One can make romanticism look silly by thinking of it as an attempt to substitute inspiration for reasoning, or as the claim that authenticity trumps argument. But in these lectures, I am trying to make both movements look good by treating them not as constructive proposals but as ways of getting out from under Platonism. (Rorty 2016, 49)

Both Romanticism and pragmatism oppose Platonism and that is what is important for Rorty: they are both attempts to escape representationalism. Nietzsche and Wittgenstein represent these attempts, Wittgenstein in a more pragmatic way and Nietzsche in a more Romantic way. But both can be said to be Romantic pragmatists in the sense that they place imagination and invention at the heart of the philosophical enterprise. Indeed, Rorty argues that Romanticism is needed if pragmatism aims to be more than a mere description:

> Whereas romanticism reminds us that imagination may produce a human future that is wonderfully different from the human present, pragmatism reminds us that the only sure test of utility is, unfortunately, retrospective – whether we, by the lights of our own time and place, are grateful to those who came up with the novel idea. If we could test for an idea's utility in advance of trying it out in practice, there would be no need for risky experimentation. But a world in which that risk is absent would be one in which we were not the finite, time-bound creatures that we are. (Rorty 2016, 56)

While pragmatism looks back to test utility, Romanticism looks forward to creating new uses. These new uses cannot be tested beforehand because the test can only occur once the uses are created. Risky experimentation, such a description reflects the importance of danger in Nietzsche's philosophy and Wittgenstein's insistence on the experimental side of inventing language-games. Nietzsche and Wittgenstein operate at the intersection between Romanticism and pragmatism thus occupying a middle ground between *Romantic Expressivism* and *Pragmatic Expressivism* that we will explore in the following chapters.

2

German philosophy of language as *Romantic Expressivism*

Ist die Sprache der adäquate Ausdruck aller Realitäten?
Friedrich Nietzsche, *On Truth and Lie*, §1

Representationalism raises two major issues: first, it has a metaphysical dimension that both Nietzsche and Wittgenstein aim to dismiss; second, it fails to account for poetic or literary uses of language. We have seen that pragmatism offers an alternative through its shift from reference to use in determining meaning. This idea does not appear with the classical pragmatists such as Charles Sanders Peirce and William James but is already an underlying thought of eighteenth- and nineteenth-century German philosophy of language, with thinkers such as Johann Georg Hamann (1730–88), Johann Gottfried von Herder (1744–1803), Wilhelm von Humboldt (1767–1835) and Georg Christoph Lichtenberg (1742–99). Michael Forster and Herman Cloeren among others have argued that analytic philosophy of language and its linguistic turn is less of a radical shift and break with tradition than a development of ideas taking their roots in eighteenth-century German philosophy. According to Cloeren, looking back at German philosophy of language prevents philosophy from falling into the same ideas as those of the logical positivists:

> What is more, thinkers of this movement cautiously avoided the one-sided conclusions of the logical positivists, according to which linguistic analysis is the only task of philosophy, and all solvable problems are left to logicians and scientists. As I will show, the German philosophers discussed in this study wisely held onto the notion that philosophy has genuine tasks to carry out in the theory of knowledge, in the history of philosophy, and in an elaboration of the transcendental function of language. (Cloeren 1988, 4)

These ideas are further developed by the early German Romantics such as Friedrich Schlegel (1772–1829) and Novalis (1772–1801). We have seen that Rorty considers pragmatism to have its roots in Romanticism, and going back to it opens ways to connect Nietzsche and Wittgenstein. The insistence of Romanticism on placing poetry at the heart of their views on language is a line of thought that Nietzsche pursues and that Heidegger further develops by considering that the task of philosophy after the end of metaphysics is to poeticize the world.

Against representationalism, these thinkers all consider expression to be the central notion for an alternative philosophy of language. Charles Taylor characterizes the opposition between representation and expression as an opposition between enframing (HLC for Hobbes-Locke-Condillac) and constitutive (HHH for Herder-Hamann-Humboldt) theories of language. Enframing theories remain within the representational framework and 'understand language within the confines of the modern representational epistemology made dominant by Descartes' (Taylor 2016, 4). In contrast, the constitutive type of theory 'gives us a picture of language as making possible new purposes, new levels of behavior, new meanings, and hence as not explicable within a framework picture of human life conceived without language' (Taylor 2016, 4). In this context, language shapes human life and is not a mere tool at the disposal of human beings. In other words, the 'HHH view' 'shows us language as the locus of different kinds of disclosure. It makes us aware of the expressive dimension and its importance. And it allows us to identify a constitutive dimension, a way in which language does not only represent, but enters into some of the realities it is "about"' (Taylor 1985, 273). Language shapes the world and does not merely mirror it.

Against the representational framework of modern epistemology characterized by Descartes and still dominant in contemporary philosophy of language, constitutive theories focus on expression:

> The claim is that our sensitivity to these issues of rightness arises out of and along with our ability to express it. This sensitivity is articulated in certain responses, including the various uses of words and articulate speech; but also, as we shall discuss more fully below, gesture, mimicry, the fashioning of images and symbols, and the like. This range of expressive activities, as we can call them, serves not only to communicate this sensitivity to others. The articulation serves just as much and equiprimordially to realize this

sensitivity in ourselves. This is at the core of Herder's 'expressivism.' (Taylor 2016, 29)

Taylor considers Herder's expressivism to offer a broader view of language than representationalism insofar as it reinscribes language in a vast array of human activities. Against the idea that language is a tool merely for communicating bits of information, expressivism considers language to be doing something and to have a disclosive force. He does not contest the existence of communication, what he also calls assertion, but argues that 'For an immense range of human speech and symbol, there is both assertion and disclosure' (Weiss and Wanderer 2010, 35). While representationalism works relatively well with assertion, it fails to account for disclosure. This point about disclosure is where Taylor's expressivism is specifically Romantic and distinguishes itself from contemporary forms of expressivism that we will explore in the next chapter.

Taylor's expressivism, insofar as it focuses on the disclosive dimension of language, can be considered a *Romantic Expressivism*:

> We've been talking about two ways of innovating, of coming to express or grasp a new meaning. One is through enactment, embodiment; and the other is through a description, like a metaphor or bodily 'seating' which allows us to make a leap. But how about a third form, the work of art, something which is neither expressive projection nor description? In a sense, the work of art was even more central to the development of Romantic expressivism (and hence to the HHH) than what I have been calling projection, or enactment. We can see this in the conception of the symbol, as opposed to the allegory, which played an important role in the aesthetic of the Romantic period, and indeed since. As described, for instance, by Goethe, the symbol was a paradigm of what I have been calling constitutive expression. (Taylor 2016, 234)

According to Taylor, there are three ways in which meanings come to existence: enactment, description and symbol. The third way, symbol, is related to the way works of art create new meanings and is central to *Romantic Expressivism*. Taylor also calls this third-way portrayal, in the sense that it is not a mere description (that would rely on some form of representation or imitation), nor enactment or embodiment (the projection of some meaning onto some gesture), but a specific way in which a work of art comes to portray or symbolize a meaning. This focus on the meaning of a work of art is one of the core features of *Romantic Expressivism*, as Nicholas Smith argues: 'In looking to the *work of art* as the paradigm locus of meaning the Romantics were not so much rejecting reason, science and rationality as responding to the distinctive capacity of expressive language to "make possible its own content"' (Reynolds et al. 2011, 152).

Constitutive expression – the heart of *Romantic Expressivism* and the 'HHH view' of meaning – is therefore closely related to creativity:

> The constitutive theory turns our attention toward the creative dimension of expression, in which, to speak paradoxically, it makes possible its own content. We can actually see this in familiar, everyday realities, but it tends to be screened out from the enframing perspective, and it took the development of constitutive theories to bring it to light. (Taylor 2016, 38)

The creative dimension of expression makes seeing things possible, whereas the enframing perspective closes these possibilities. Taylor rephrases here the Romantic notion of disclosure that considers creative uses of language to disclose aspects of the world that were until then hidden.

The aim of this chapter is to reconstruct the historical line of *Romantic Expressivism* that takes birth in eighteenth-century German philosophy of language and is epitomized in Heidegger's poetic philosophy. This history establishes the grounds on which Nietzsche and Wittgenstein can be related to one another, as both belonging to a form of expressivism. It further establishes the background against which contemporary forms of expressivism, that I will explore in the next chapter as *Pragmatic Expressivism*, can be contrasted, thus relating Nietzsche and Wittgenstein to contemporary concerns in philosophy of language.

1 From representation to expression: The 'HHH view of meaning'

In their own ways, Herder, Hamann, Humboldt and Lichtenberg all argue against a metaphysical conception of language – that is, a language in which meanings would have a fixed essence – and elaborate a conception of language as being historically constructed. Taylor considers the first three to form the 'HHH view' of meaning in which representation does not play the primary role. As Forster argues, they consider that 'meaning or concepts are [...] *usages of words*' (Forster 2010, 16). If meanings are provided by usage, there is no need for a metaphysical conception of language as language is established in practice and not fixed by a divine authority. This shift from reference to use reflects the opposition between Cratylus and Hermogenes mentioned in Chapter 1: the origin of language is not a divine projection but human conventions and agreements. As we will see in the next chapters, quite a few elements of this tradition find their way into Nietzsche's and Wittgenstein's philosophies, the most striking being found in what has been epitomized as Wittgenstein's – and the ordinary language philosophers' – so-called 'meaning as use' conception. Even though there is much more to Ordinary Language Philosophy than this mere replacement of reference by use, this shift in focus from the metaphysical object 'language' (whose characteristics can vary) to a practice (or a set of practices) is central. Such a conception leads not only to understanding language as a convention (the rules of usage) but also as a creation. (Language evolves, and new language uses can be created.) It is this idea of creation that opens a space for poetic language. Rather than being metaphysically fixed, language is considered as something dynamic, as an always-evolving practice.

When looking back at this supposed origin of language, Herder expresses critical views on the development of language:

> *In all original languages remains of these natural sounds still resound* – only, to be sure, they are not the main threads of human language. They are not the actual roots, but the juices which enliven the roots of language.
>
> In a refined, late-invented metaphysical language, which is a degeneration, perhaps at the fourth degree, from the original savage mother [tongue] of the human species, and which after long millennia of degeneration has itself in turn for centuries of its life been refined, civilized, and humanized – such a language, the child of reason and society, can know little or nothing any more about the childhood of its first mother. But the old, the savage, languages, the nearer they are to the origin, the more of it they contain. I cannot here yet speak of the slightest *human* formation [*Bildung*] of language, but can only consider raw materials. There does not yet exist for me any word, but only sounds towards the word for a sensation. (Herder 2002, 68)

As we will see, Nietzsche's early (and even later) views on language are very close to those of Herder, even though he expresses some dissent with them.

Herder criticizes metaphysical language as a degeneration from the original language of sounds. Language is metaphysical in the sense that it fixes an essence for the things it designates: when language evolves, there is no longer a link between the sound and the object but only a fixed convention, what Nietzsche calls a fixation of metaphors into concepts. Language in this sense is a social construct and not the result of a natural development. This criticism of the metaphysical conception of language is one of the central points of contact between analytic and continental philosophies, even though analytic philosophers will not follow the view according to which language has a sensuous origin. There is something unnatural about language that is deceitful, such as Herder's claim. Nietzsche will follow it to some extent, and analytic philosophers will adopt a similar stance but for other reasons. Indeed, for Wittgenstein among others, the problem does not reside in the unnaturalness of language but in its metaphysical character, in the fact that words are taken out of their ordinary use and employed in a metaphysical way, that is, using them as if they were giving an account of the essence of things (whereas they are, as Herder says, refined at 'the fourth degree', very far from the things themselves). Metaphysical language thus relies on the idea that language does not only represent the world but also accounts for the essence of things: metaphysics relies on representationalism.

Hamann offers views similar to those of Herder and brings into question the origin and the nature of language, again in relation to a critique of metaphysics.[1] He also believes language and thought to be closely linked, and he argues in his *Essay on an Academic Question* that language is defined as a way of communicating thoughts: 'Since the concept of that which is understood by "language" is of such diverse meaning, it would be best to determine it according to its purpose as the means to communicate our thoughts and to understand the thoughts of others' (Hamann 2007, 17). Underlying such a conception of language is the dependence between thought and language; thoughts cannot be expressed with any other means than language. Hamann also brings to the fore the communicative nature of language which does not entail a functionalist conception of language as a tool but insists on the fact that language is essentially something shared and used to share thoughts. We find here a basic understanding of language as a social practice which will grow into an important conception of language in the later Wittgenstein and in Ordinary Language Philosophy.[2]

This conception of language as a social practice entails a critique of metaphysical language. Indeed, as Hamann states in *Aesthetic in Nuce*:

> To speak is to translate – from an angelic language into a human language, that is, to translate thoughts into words, – things into names – images into signs, which can be poetic or curiological, historic or symbolic or hieroglyphic – and philosophical or characteristic. This kind of translation (that is, speech) resembles more than anything else the wrong side of a tapestry. (Hamann 2007, 66)

According to Hamann, speech is a kind of translation which can occur at different levels (names, signs, etc.). To some extent, this view of levels of translation can be linked to Herder's conception of a metaphysical language refined 'at the fourth degree'. The translation creates a distance between things and names. Whereas a metaphysical language considers the link between the name and the object to be a direct one, for Hamann a translation takes place in speech. Hamann criticizes what Samuel Wheeler calls a 'magic language', that is, a self-interpreting language in which there is no need for interpretation or, in Hamann's words, translation (Wheeler 2000). In this sense, a 'magic language' is transparent: everything is crystal clear, meanings and interpretation are given and do not need to be found.[3] A 'magic language' relies on the prejudice that language is metaphysical and that there is therefore a direct link from word to thing, from meaning to essence. Hamann works against such a conception of language, and the importance he gives to translation reveals the interpretative dimension of language that will be central to Friedrich Schleiermacher and the hermeneutic tradition. This translation can take different forms (poetic, historic, philosophical, etc.). This notion of translation, as Herder's notion of refinement 'at the fourth degree', will be developed by Nietzsche's notions of metaphor and concept in TL. Although I will discuss Nietzsche's conception of language more extensively in Chapter 4, it is already interesting to point out the relation between translation (*Übersetzung*) and metaphor (*Metapher* but also *Übertragung*). In Hamann's translation as much as in Nietzsche's metaphor, language is perceived as operating a move from perception to word (and later to the concept).

This shift from words to concepts appears in Hamann's later works where, even though his conception of language slightly changes, the main idea of translation remains. In the *Metacritique of Pure Reason*, he answers to Kant and argues:

> Words, therefore, have an aesthetic and logical faculty. As visible and audible objects they belong with their elements to the sensibility and intuition; however, by the spirit of their institution and meaning, they belong to the understanding and concepts. Consequently, words are pure and empirical intuitions as much as pure and empirical concepts. Empirical, because the sensation of vision or hearing is effected through them; pure, inasmuch as their meaning is determined by nothing that belongs to those sensations. Words as the undetermined objects of empirical intuitions are entitled, in the original text of pure reason, aesthetic appearances; therefore, according to the endlessly repeated antithetical parallelism, words as undetermined objects of empirical concepts are entitled critical appearances, specters, non-words or unwords, and become determinate objects for the understanding only through their institution and meaning in usage. This meaning and its determination arises, as everyone knows, from the combination of a word-sign, which is *a priori* arbitrary and indifferent and *a posteriori* necessary and indispensable, with the intuition of the word itself; through this reiterated bond the concept is communicated to, imprinted on, and incorporated in the understanding, by means of the word-sign as by the intuition itself. (Hamann 2007, 215–16)

Hamann characterizes words as two-sided. On the one hand, they are translations from empirical intuitions, from the perception of a thing to the sound of the word, and this gives words their aesthetic faculty: they are objects (or sounds) with a specific form. On the other hand, they are concepts; they have a meaning which is unrelated to the original empirical intuition (or only 'at the fourth degree') that provides the logical faculty of the word. These two faculties are bound together in words: the intuition of the world and the arbitrary word-sign that designates it, prefiguring in some sense Ferdinand de Saussure's conception of the arbitrary of the sign that will be very influential in structuralist and post-structuralist thought (Saussure 2011, 67–70).

This arbitrariness of words and the lack of relation between the word-sign and the intuition lead Hamann to a critique of metaphysics:

> Metaphysics abuses the word-signs and figures of speech of our empirical knowledge by treating them as nothing but hieroglyphs and types of ideal relations. Through this learned troublemaking it works the honest decency of language into such a meaningless, rutting, unstable, indefinite something = X that nothing is left but a windy sough, a magic shadow play, at most, as the wise Helvétius says, the talisman and rosary of a transcendental

superstitious belief in *entia rationis*, their empty sacks and slogans. (Hamann 2007, 210)

Hamann's critique of metaphysics is thus mainly focused on the use (or abuse) of word-signs as concepts. The fixed and arbitrary meaning distances itself from the empirical intuitions and, in the end, detaches itself completely. Metaphysics considers word-signs as 'hieroglyphs', as abstract ideas, and thus turn language into something meaningless. Behind the equation 'something = X' lies nothing but abstract ideas. Hamann's critique of metaphysics can be linked not only to Nietzsche's critique of the 'thing-in-itself' and of the 'true world' but also to Wittgenstein's critique of the way philosophers consider some words as being more important, more special than others, as we have seen in the previous chapter.

Like Herder and Hamann from whom he inherits, Humboldt attempts to escape representationalism. As James Underhill argues, Humboldt does not consider language to be a mere vehicle for thought nor a mirror of the world (Underhill 2009, 49). Following this idea, one of the main aspects of Humboldt's view of language is that he 'conceptualised language not as a fixed, unchanging thing but as a living process' (Underhill 2009, 50). To that extent, Humboldt pursues Herder's and Hamann's thoughts but focuses and develops further the idea of language as an evolving process.

For Humboldt, language is an activity which keeps evolving:

> *Language*, regarded in its real nature, is an enduring thing, and at every moment a *transitory* one. Even its maintenance by writing is always just an incomplete, mummy-like preservation, only needed again in attempting thereby to picture the living utterance. In itself it is no product (*Ergon*), but an activity (*Energeia*). Its true definition can therefore only be a genetic one. (Humboldt 1999, 49)

Like Herder and Hamann, Humboldt considers language as a practice. To that extent, he focuses on the notion of speech rather than writing. Whether speech is really a more fundamental mode or use of language than writing is not the question here. What is important is that language is a *transitory* activity. Language is meant to evolve and to change and is certainly not to be fixed as an eternal entity. Concepts are not *aeternae veritates* and a definition of language 'can therefore only be a genetic one' or, following Nietzsche's vocabulary, a genealogical one: language must be grasped in its uses and in its history.

Although not included in Taylor's 'HHH view', Lichtenberg is another eighteenth-century German philosopher whose influence on both Nietzsche and Wittgenstein is attested. Wittgenstein's comments about his readings are often scarce, but, as Allan Janik and Stephen Toulmin argue: 'One of the few philosophical writers who impressed him from early on was Georg Christoph Lichtenberg' (Janik and Toulmin 1996, 176). As for Nietzsche, Thomas Brobjer shows that 'Georg Christoph Lichtenberg is one of the only two German philosophers and thinkers (the other being Lessing) toward whom Nietzsche had a positive attitude throughout his development' (Brobjer 2008, 63). Lichtenberg too was a critic of metaphysics and considered language as the central matter of philosophy. More than just being a shared historical source for Nietzsche and Wittgenstein, Lichtenberg also raises some important metaphilosophical questions, especially those of the aim and scope of philosophy and of the writing of philosophy itself.

Both Nietzsche and Wittgenstein have an interest in Lichtenberg's writings, and the relation between this concern and their philosophy of language is expressed at its best in one of Lichtenberg's sentence from note 146, book H of his *The Waste Books*: 'Our whole philosophy is rectification of colloquial linguistic usage, thus rectification of a philosophy, and indeed of the most universal and general' (Lichtenberg 1990, 122). This sentence is important because there is evidence that it was read by both Nietzsche and Wittgenstein. Indeed, Nietzsche underlines 'rectification of colloquial linguistic usage' in his copy of the book and, as Martin Stingelin notes in his study of Nietzsche's Lichtenberg reception, shares with Lichtenberg his understanding of critique of language as critique of concepts (Stingelin 1996, 103). And Wittgenstein quotes this sentence in section 90 of the *Big Typescript*. This idea of philosophy as rectification of language prefigures the linguistic turn and inspires Nietzsche and Wittgenstein.

Lichtenberg's focus on the use of language differs from the view held by Herder and Hamann. The question is no longer about the relation of meaning to linguistic usage but about linguistic usage itself as being in need of rectification. With Lichtenberg, the study of language takes a metaphilosophical turn: a concern with language leads to a concern with the nature of philosophical activity. Language is not only an object of philosophical inquiry but also the means by which this inquiry is carried out. As such, a reflection about language becomes a reflection about the linguistic nature of philosophy. This questioning about the nature of philosophical activity is obviously linked to a critique of metaphysics as traditionally conceived on the grounds of language, as Lichtenberg's critique of the Cartesian 'I think' reveals. In the fragment K 76 from *The Waste Books*, Lichtenberg considers Descartes presupposition of the 'I' in 'I think': 'We know only the existence of our sensations, representations, and thoughts. *It thinks*, we should say, just as we say, *it lightnings*. To say *cogito* is already too much if we translate it as *I think*. To assume the *I*, to postulate it, is a practical necessity' (Lichtenberg 2012, 152). Before the existence of ourselves, Lichtenberg considers that we know our 'sensations, representations, and thoughts'. He operates an inversion of Descartes's *cogito* which reconsiders the whole of Descartes's metaphysics. John Campbell compares Lichtenberg's critique of the *cogito* to Wittgenstein's 'reports of immediate experience' and considers that Wittgenstein operates a similar move (Campbell 2012, 368). Nietzsche pursues a similar interpretation in BGE and considers that the postulation of the 'I' is a 'grammatical habit' (BGE 17 / KSA 5.31). Such a conception of philosophy and language requires rethinking how philosophy ought to be expressed. Lichtenberg is a perfect example of that: for him, philosophical writing involves writing as such. The 'linguistic usage' concerns Lichtenberg in two ways: in his analysis of language on the one hand and on his use of language, that is his style, on the other hand. Through his thinking about language, Lichtenberg brings to the fore the metaphilosophical questions of the nature and expression of philosophy.

Nietzsche and Wittgenstein share this metaphilosophical concern with Lichtenberg, which shows in their specific ways of writing, in their styles, that share with Lichtenberg the aphoristic dimension. In his introduction to Lichtenberg's *The Waste Books*, R. J. Hollingdale argues that one should be cautious in taking this aphoristic connection as a means to compare Lichtenberg, Nietzsche and Wittgenstein as there are important stylistic differences among them.[4] However, this use of the fragmentary form reveals a shared concern with the use of language and its impact on philosophy itself. The turn to language entails a turn to the language of philosophy. By questioning the nature of philosophy, they must take into consideration the form of philosophy and thus tackle the question 'what form should philosophy take?' After Herder, Hamann, Humboldt and Lichtenberg, the German Romantics tackled these questions about the nature of philosophy and its relation to poetry.

2 The poetic view: Friedrich Schlegel and the German Romantics

The German Romantics inherit from the ideas explored earlier and further develop the relation between language and poetry. In this section, I will focus especially on Friedrich Schlegel and Novalis as their ideas will be quite influential on Nietzsche. A first element can be found in the German Romantics' concern with the notion of fragment, thus developing the thought expressed with Lichtenberg. The German Romantics develop an aesthetics of the fragment which has a complex relation to the systematic form in philosophy, and, as Elizabeth Millan-Zaibert argues, the Romantics' concept of the fragment is a way of escaping an artificial system which would impose a structure upon a plurality of ideas.[5]

To illustrate this complex relation, Schlegel holds a dual view on systems: he considers his method based on the life of thought to be a system (in the sense of an organic system) but not in the negative sense according to which 'systematic coherence is only external and specious' (Schlegel 1855, 347). He distinguishes between organic systems produced and determined by life and systems built by philosophers who impose an external force to hold the things together. Nietzsche takes up this rejection of systems and systematic philosophy, and his attitude towards the system is summarized in TI: 'I mistrust all systematists and avoid them' (TI 'Arrows' 26 / KSA 6.63). The notion of mistrust suggests that systems often hide something, that their attempt to structure reality might only be an artifice.

For both Nietzsche and Schlegel, the attack on the notion of system is related to their rejection of Hegel and the tradition of German Idealism, and especially of its systematic style. Schlegel's writing in fragments and Nietzsche's writing in aphorisms do reveal an attempt to write philosophy differently, in a radically different way from Hegel's system.[6] This search for a different expression leads the German Romantics and Nietzsche to favour a literary form, and, as Millan-Zaibert notes, 'philosophers continue to underestimate the role of literary form in philosophy, which hinders an appreciation of the philosophical contributions of the early German Romantics' (Millan-Zaibert 2007, 45–6). The inclusion of poetry and literature in the realm of philosophy reconfigures the language of philosophy itself. In contrast to the systematic form that reveals an external coherence, the literary form used by the German

Romantics and Nietzsche reveals an internal coherence, similar to that of an organic system.

This reflection on system and the inclusion of poetry within the philosophical realm shows Schlegel's concern with language and its relation to the world. This concern also serves as ground for his questioning of the relation between philosophy, poetry and truth – and to a larger extent the relation between art and science. His lecture 'Philosophy of Language' focuses on the relation between language and life (and therefore art, as art is an integral part of life for him). His conception of language follows in part that of Herder and Hamann. Indeed, he too considers that 'there is, then, an intrinsic connection between thought and speech, between language and consciousness' (Schlegel 1855, 425). Because of this connection, language plays an important role in different domains of human activity: 'living thought and the science thereof, can not well or easily be separated from the philosophy of language' (Schlegel 1855, 425). This foundational role of language in another science (or another domain of philosophy) is a key element to the philosophical developments in the 'linguistic turn'. Following Herder and Hamann, Schlegel reinforces the place and role of language in philosophy. As we have seen with Lichtenberg, to place language back in philosophy entails rethinking the writing (or the style) of philosophy. Schlegel takes up this metaphilosophical concern and pushes it further. Denis Thouard goes as far as saying that 'thinking the textuality of philosophy becomes a philosophical problem with [Schlegel]'[7] (Thouard 2001). We might nuance this claim in regard to what we have said about Lichtenberg, but Schlegel most certainly brings this reflection on philosophical style to the fore.

Novalis holds a similar view of the relation between language and world. For instance, he states in the *Logological Fragments* that 'Everything we experience is a *communication*. Thus the world is indeed a *communication* – a revelation of the spirit. The age has passed when the spirit of God could be understood. The meaning of the world is lost. We have stopped at the letter. As a result of the appearance we have lost that which is appearing. Formulary beings' (Novalis 1997, 81, emphasis in original). The importance given to communication and the understanding of this communication through the understanding of language brings to the fore the metaphilosophical dimension of philosophical reflection: 'The history of philosophy up to now is nothing but a history of attempts to discover how to do philosophy' (Novalis 1997, 47). This metareflective character also appears in Novalis's conception of language. In the 'Monologue', he argues that the whole point of language is to be concerned with itself: 'It is amazing, the absurd error people make of imagining they are speaking for the sake of things; no one knows the essential thing about language, that it is concerned only with itself' (Bernstein 2003, 214). Language does not refer to things in the world, but only to itself. This conception, however, leads to an ironic comment from Novalis: 'And though I believe that with these words I have delineated the nature and office of poetry as clearly as I can, all the same I know that no one can understand it, and what I have said is quite foolish because I wanted to say it, and that is no way for poetry to come about' (Bernstein 2003, 215). If language only refers to itself, poetry – understood as the mastery of language – can only express the nature of language, and any attempt to describe the nature of poetry is therefore an attempt to describe the nature of language, a task which runs in circle.

The Romantics' and Nietzsche's distrust of systems and systematic writing comes, among other things, from the rejection of the correspondence theory of truth. This rejection is linked to their critique of metaphysics and their new conception of language. If language is not 'magic', if meanings are not given but call for interpretation, language cannot be considered as the exact representation of the world anymore. Once the direct link between language and world is taken down, the whole theory of truth as correspondence collapses as well. Truth (and meaning) cannot be considered as a matter of correspondence between a statement and a fact because the statement enters in the constitution of the fact; language takes part in elaborating the world. As Forster rightfully notes, Schlegel here 'anticipates aspects of Nietzsche's perspectivism' (Forster 2011, 30). Andrew Bowie similarly suggests that German Romantics anticipate the Nietzschean question of truth: 'The Romantic understanding of truth both prefigures Nietzsche's question and implies that any determinate answer to it, for example, in terms of power as the ground of truth, fails to understand the real nature of truth' (Bowie 1997, 73). Nietzsche's questioning of the value we give to truth is based on his conception of language. A different conception of language (one tending towards literature and denying a 'magic language') calls for a rethinking of truth and how to express it, in a way that resembles literary expression.

In such a context, philosophy and poetry become closer to one another, and Schlegel even considers that 'poetry and philosophy should be made one' (Bernstein 2003, 244). This bringing together of poetry and philosophy (understood as science) is well expressed in *Anathaeum Fragments* 255:

> The more poetry becomes science, the more it also becomes art. If poetry is to become art, if the artist is to have a thorough understanding and knowledge of his ends and means, his difficulties and his subjects, then the poet will have to philosophize about his art. If he is to be more than a mere contriver and artisan, if he is to be an expert in his field and understand his fellow citizens in the kingdom of art, then he will have to become a philologist as well. (Bernstein 2003, 54)

For poetry to become art to its full extent, it must include a philosophical reflection on itself. In the Romantic framework, it is only through philosophy that poetry can become fully conscious of itself, of its ends and means, of what it ought to do and be.

This philosophical dimension is, however, not the only one needed: Schlegel also adds philology; not only must the poet be a philosopher, but he must be a philologist as well. This notion of philology occupies the young Schlegel as his notes on *Philosophy of Philology* reveal. He attempts to rethink philology by adding a stronger critical and historical component. For Schlegel, poetry, philosophy and philology must work together, and 'One has to be born for philology just as for poetry and philosophy'. This triad – poetry, philosophy and philology – prefigures some of the Nietzschean developments. In Nietzsche's works as well, poetry, philosophy and philology work together. Philology is important as the art of reading well (and to this extent interpreting). As he says at the end of the preface to D, to read well (as a philologist) is to read slowly or to ruminate as he names this activity in GM. The importance of poetry (and to a wider extent art) appears throughout all of Nietzsche's works, and TSZ even takes the form of a poem. Poetry and philology thus affect Nietzsche's conception of philosophy: poetry has an impact on his style and philology brings into focus the notion of interpretation.

Novalis understands the relation between philosophy and poetry in a similar way: 'Poetry is the hero of philosophy. Philosophy raises poetry to the status of a principle. It teaches us to recognize the worth of poetry.

Philosophy is *the theory of poetry*. It shows us what poetry is, that is one and all' (Novalis 1997, 79). What poetry brings to the fore is the idea of creation which Nietzsche will extensively develop. Novalis already argues that 'Writing poetry is creating' (Novalis 1997, 55). This notion of creating brings to the fore the idea that poetry is not a closed category which, for instance, would refer to all versified texts (and Aristotle already suggests that Heredotus's work put into verse would still be history[8]) – it is not a subcategory of literature – but describes a more general dimension which encompasses all the arts. The use of the term 'Poesie' rather than 'Dichtung' goes back to the etymological roots of the word, the Greek '*poiesis*' which means to make or to create. Rather than establishing a closed genre, the German Romantics open the notion of poetry to encompass all creative works. This notion of creation is central to Nietzsche's philosophy, and, in Romantic terms, Nietzsche's philosophy is a poetic one insofar as it is a philosophy of creation. The Romantics' efforts to put aesthetics and poetics at the centre of philosophical concerns is an important step not only to understand Nietzsche's philosophy but also to create a ground on which Nietzsche and Wittgenstein can meet. As Bowie argues, there is a 'Romantic connection' (Bowie 2000) between analytic and continental philosophy, and this connection can bring Nietzsche and Wittgenstein closer to one another.[9] Friedrich Schlegel and the early German Romantics bring to the fore reflections that Nietzsche will take up in his works. One of the central aspects of the Romantic enterprise is the attempt to reconfigure the relation between philosophy and poetry (and to a wider extent between philosophy and art). The poetic and the aesthetic acquire a central role, and Nietzsche will pursue these lines of inquiry. Further than Nietzsche, Heidegger takes on this idea and considers poetry almost on par with philosophy after the end of metaphysics.

3 Heidegger and the rule of poetry

One of the reasons for Heidegger's shift from philosophy to poetry is that he considers that philosophy is metaphysics. Its end therefore brings philosophers to rethink their task. For him, 'Metaphysics thinks beings as a whole – the world, man, God – with respect to Being, with respect to the belonging together of beings in Being' (Heidegger 1977, 374). Many aspects are at play in such a definition, and I will point out two: (1) metaphysics is a globalizing or totalizing approach, and it is an attempt at thinking the whole and the parts as parts of this whole; (2) such an approach refers to a unified principle. Metaphysics could thus be defined as an understanding of the whole under a unified principle (such as Platonic Ideas and the Hegelian 'Absolute Spirit'). Heidegger considers that metaphysics has reached its end because a fundamental dimension of philosophy opened by the Greeks has reached its completion: 'the development of sciences' which 'is at the same time their separation from philosophy and the establishment of their independence' (Heidegger 1977, 375). The development of sciences and their total independence from philosophy has led metaphysics to its completion. In other words, if philosophy as metaphysics is an attempt at defining or determining what the world is, science is better at achieving such a task. Although at first one and the same, science is now separated from philosophy, and this split marks the end of metaphysics: if philosophy is not science anymore, what is its task?

Nietzsche also brings this question to the fore, noticing the importance science takes over philosophy:

> Running the risk that moralizing, even my own, will prove to be what it always has been (an unabashed *montrer ses plaies*, according to Balzac), I would like to try to argue against an unseemly and harmful hierarchical shift between science and philosophy that is now threatening to develop quite unnoticed and, it seems, in good conscience. [. . .] Science is abloom these days, its good conscience shining from its face, while recent philosophy has gradually sunk to its dregs, awakening distrust and despondence if not scorn and pity. Philosophy reduced to a 'theory of cognition,' really no more than a shy epochism and doctrine of renunciation; a philosophy that doesn't even get beyond the threshold, scrupulously *refusing* itself the right to enter: this is philosophy at its last gasp, an end, an agony, something to evoke pity. How could a philosophy like that – *be the master*! (BGE 204 / KSA 5.131-132)

With the rise of science, philosophy must reinvent itself. It cannot do metaphysics anymore and should not, according to Nietzsche, follow what science does. Like Heidegger, Nietzsche considers the necessity for philosophy to find its task at the end of metaphysics, and this task should not look towards science. This brings us to a question Heidegger raises in discussing the end of metaphysics: 'What task is reserved for thinking at the end of philosophy?' (Heidegger 1977, 373).

Heidegger uses the word thinking to characterize this non-metaphysical philosophy.[10] What task remains for thinking? 'A thinking which can be neither metaphysics nor science?'(Heidegger 1977, 378). The task of thinking and the reflection on the task of thinking becomes one of Heidegger's main concerns. The subtitle to his *Introduction to Philosophy: Thinking and Poetizing* reveals this shift in philosophical thought. Once philosophy is distinguished from metaphysics and from the natural sciences, the task of philosophy or thinking changes. One of Heidegger's insights in this change will be to turn towards the poetic because of the linguistic nature of philosophy. One of the central elements in his reshaped philosophy is language, and this will lead him to the question of poetry. Heidegger operates here a linguistic turn, which leads to a poetic turn.

Heidegger considers poetry as the original language, as the place where all language is created and thereby follows the Romantics. This consideration of poetry as original language appears for instance at the end of his lectures on *Logic as the Question Concerning the Essence of Language* (Heidegger 2009, 145). In these lectures, he considers the study of logic (in the etymological sense of *logos*) as being essentially a study of language. More specifically, the study of logic leads to a questioning of the essence of language as 'philosophizing is nothing else than the constant being underway in the fore-field of the fore-questions' (Heidegger 2009, 19). According to Heidegger, logic is a science that sprang out of philosophy, like the other sciences. The question of logic is a philosophical question and not a scientific one as 'philosophy is other than science' (Heidegger 2009, 18). A questioning of logic leads to a philosophical questioning of language, which must be distinguished from a scientific questioning because following the ways of natural sciences does not let us out of logic itself.

> Finally, the moment we attempt to ask about language, following the way of natural science, we run against the dictionary and grammar – in order, then, to ascertain that all of grammar derives itself from the Greek logic, which determines the fundamental concepts and rules of speaking and saying. We get in the strange position that we, on the one hand, free ourselves from logic only to arrive, on the other hand, again in the fetters of logic. (Heidegger 2009, 18)

A scientific questioning of language only brings us back to our starting point, logic. On the contrary, a philosophical inquiry leads us to a questioning of the essence of language. In the course of his lectures, the questioning of logic leads in turn to language, human being, history and poetry. From the question of logic, and because of his definition of it, Heidegger moves to the question of poetry.[11]

In *On the Essence of Language*, Heidegger agrees with Herder on turning away from logic. But according to Heidegger, Herder misses the turning away from the metaphysics of language: '*The turning away from "logic"* is certainly correct, and yet he remains stuck in the *logos* of reason, of the formation of marks, and supplements everything only from the economy of nature' (Heidegger 2004, 71). In order to move away from this metaphysical conception of language (in which words refer to things and truth can be thought in terms of correspondence), Heidegger turns towards poetry as 'The poem has no "content"' (Heidegger 2004, 60). This lack of content calls for a rethinking of language, in other terms than metaphysics or science. As Heidegger argues in *On the Way to Language*: 'scientific and philosophical information about language is one thing; an experience we undergo with language is another' (Heidegger 1982, 59). This experience of language has something to do with poetry, and through his thinking about language, Heidegger rethinks the relation between philosophy and poetry, bringing them closer to one another. This opposition between scientific language and linguistic experience reflects the opposition between the programme of analysis and that of pragmatism, as we will see in the next chapter. In that framework, the early Heidegger has been considered as a kind of pragmatist, and some connections have been highlighted between Heidegger and Wittgenstein (Apel 1967; Braver 2012). However, a crucial difference remains between Heidegger and pragmatists which can be seen in Heidegger consideration of poetic language as the origin of language. This difference reflects the difference between *Romantic Expressivism* and contemporary *Pragmatic Expressivism* that will be the focus of the next chapter.

According to Heidegger, the common ground between philosophy and poetry is language (*Sprache*) and both say (*Sagen*) what there is. 'Sinnen' and 'Sagen' are the two characteristics shared by both domains. In his notes towards writing 'Denken und Dichten' Heidegger formulates this link more clearly: '*Thinking and poetizing* – each time a meditation [*Sinnen*], each time a saying: the reflective word. The thinkers and the poets, the ones who reflectively speak and the ones who verbally reflect' (Heidegger 2011, 59). Heidegger plays with the word *Sinnen*, translated here as 'mediation', that shares root with *Sinn*, 'sense' or 'meaning', also with a connotation of 'direction'. In his foreword to his translation, Phillip Jacques Braunstein explains the meaning of *Sinnen* as a 'thought that pursues a certain path' (Heidegger 2011, xi). Poets and philosophers alike make sense and say it. The difference between them is a matter of focus: on *Sinnen* for philosophers and on *Sagen* for poets. But the core matter is the same for philosophy and poetry: language. This is the reason why Heidegger considers philosophy to be closer to poetry than to any other art: 'Yet thinking and poetizing reveal an even closer relation [*Verwandtschaft*] than thinking and painting. Thinking and poetizing exist exclusively in the realm of language. Their works and only theirs are of a linguistic "nature"' (Heidegger 2011, 44).

Because of this common 'linguistic nature', philosophy and poetry are two neighbouring domains which define (or in a milder way reflect about) themselves through one another. Thinking needs poetry as much as poetry needs thinking. Philosophy and poetry relate to one another and, in this relation, modify their views. The borders between these two domains are never fixed; they are always changing as they affect each other, and their definitions are dialectically constructed through their relations. The aim of thinking is close to that of poetry as they both bring our attention to saying and by doing so making sense ('*Sinnen*'). Heidegger follows the path of the poetic experience with language against the scientific study of language. This concern with art and poetry as core matters for philosophy contrasts sharply with philosophers who focus on science and logic such as the logical positivists and shows that Heidegger belongs to the Romantic tradition explored earlier.

It is, however, questionable whether *Romantic Expressivism* brings metaphysics to an end. Indeed, there are two aspects of their philosophy of language that seem to retain a metaphysical dimension. First, the idea of disclosure suggests that there is something hidden to disclose, perhaps of the kind of the metaphysical true world that Nietzsche criticizes. It suggests that there is a reality beyond or behind the veil of the appearances, behind our everyday language. Second, related to the first point, there is a sacralization of poetry that leaves the ordinary aside. Whereas ordinary language philosophers reject poetic uses of language as deviances, *Romantic Expressivism* seems to consider these uses to be the heart of language, thus leaving ordinary language aside. In both cases, there is a devaluation of certain uses of language, the poetic for the enframing (HLC) view and the ordinary for the constitutive (HHH) view, a criticism that Nietzsche already suggests when he says:

> Conversely, the high estimation for the 'most important things' is almost never wholly genuine: the priests and metaphysicians have admittedly gotten us completely accustomed to a hypocritically exaggerated *use of language* in these areas, and yet not changed the tune of our feeling that these most important things are not to be taken to be as important as those disdained nearby things. (WS 5 / KSA2.541)

In a sense, *Romantic Expressivism* is still playing the game of priests and metaphysicians as they exaggerate poetic use of language. In its attempt to balance metaphysics, *Romantic Expressivism* falls back into a metaphysics of a different kind. A philosophy of language should not exaggerate the importance of 'important things' and should therefore not disdain 'nearby things'.

3

Pragmatic Expressivism
Brandom, Price, Blackburn

We have seen that expressivism refers to a certain tradition in German philosophy of language. However, this notion refers to a substantially different tradition in contemporary debates, pointing to a group of philosophers including Robert Brandom, Huw Price and Simon Blackburn among others.[1] According to Price, 'The term "expressivism" is often introduced via the proposal that the function of certain claims (or apparent claims) is (i) not to *describe* some aspect of the world but rather (ii) to *express* a psychological state (other than a belief) – an affective state, say)' (Price 2019, 133–4). Price argues that only the first claim is necessary, and expressivism is therefore not limited to affective states but is a more global take on how language works: some/all statements do not represent the world but express it.[2] Although contemporary expressivism does not endorse the full Romantic programme, especially not its suspicion towards rationality and its conception of truth as disclosure, this schematic account already shows some insightful connections, related to the breadth of Brandom's investigation according to Nicholas Smith. Indeed, Smith argues, Brandom coins the term 'expressivism', 'as a label not just for his own project, but for a whole philosophical tradition that encompasses thinkers as diverse as Kant, Hegel, the American pragmatists, Heidegger and Wittgenstein' (Reynolds et al. 2011, 145). This broad view gives historical roots to expressivism and connects it to pragmatism. I will therefore call contemporary expressivism *Pragmatic Expressivism*, in contrast to *Romantic Expressivism*. In moving from Romanticism to pragmatism, *Pragmatic Expressivism* avoids some of the metaphysical aspects that underlie the Romantic programme, but also lose some grasp on poetry. The aim of this chapter is to give an account of *Pragmatic Expressivism* as it can be found in the works of Brandom, Price and Blackburn. Despite the attractiveness of *Pragmatic Expressivism*, I will argue in this chapter that the best conception of expressivism is to be found in the Nietzsche-Wittgenstein connection, which I will outline in the next chapter. In other words, *Romantic Expressivism* would gain from more Wittgenstein while *Pragmatic Expressivism* would gain from more Nietzsche.

There are four parts in this chapter, which form a circle from the Romantics back to Nietzsche through Brandom, Price and Blackburn. The first part focuses on the relation between *Pragmatic Expressivism* and the Romantic tradition. While there are some clear points of contact, there are also points of disagreement. The heritage from the German tradition in philosophy of language (especially in Brandom's works) is mediated through pragmatism, and this mediation brings to a different picture of language. The second part explores *Pragmatic Expressivism* and discusses its main characteristics and features. The opposition to representationalism is one of the important aspects, but the outputs of *Pragmatic Expressivism* outgrow mere critique. The third part turns to the limits of *Pragmatic Expressivism*, showing that the differences between Brandom, Price and Blackburn reveal that there still is a form of attachment to representation (and hence to metaphysics). One of the main problems of *Pragmatic Expressivism* is the idea that language has a downtown (contra Wittgenstein) and that this downtown is a privileged point of view. The fourth and final part connects *Pragmatic Expressivism* to Nietzsche through the notion of perspectivism. The idea of vocabulary that Brandom takes from Rorty reflects in some sense Nietzsche's perspectivism but brings it in a different direction.

1 From Romanticism to pragmatism

As mentioned earlier, Brandom inscribes his expressivism in the history of philosophy and roots it in what he calls a broad pragmatism, which includes the classical American pragmatists such as Peirce and James but also the early Heidegger and the later Wittgenstein.[3] As we have seen in Chapter 1, this broad pragmatism offers a space in which so-called analytic and so-called continental philosophers can meet. Brandom further considers himself to actualize some aspects of Hegel's philosophy, which can seem surprising insofar as analytic philosophy was born out of the rejection of the Hegelian-influenced British Idealism. By connecting his work to Hegel, Brandom indirectly relates it to the German philosophy of language explored in Chapter 2, even though the relation between Hegel and the Romantics is a complex one. Indeed, while Brandom acknowledges his proximity to Hegel, he however considers himself to follow a route different from that of the Romantics (and even of traditional pragmatists).

> The original Romantic expressivists were (like the pragmatists, both classical and contemporary) *assimilationists* about the conceptual. My way of working out an expressivist approach is *exceptionalist*, focusing on the differentiae distinctive of the conceptual as such. It is a *rationalist* pragmatism, in giving pride of place to practices of giving and asking for reasons, understanding them as conferring conceptual content on performances, expressions, and states suitably caught up in those practices. [. . .] And it is a rationalist expressivism in that it understands *expressing* something, making it *explicit*, as putting it in a form in which it can both serve as and stand in need of *reasons:* a form in which it can serve as both premise and conclusion in *inferences.* (Brandom 2003, 10–11)

The key concept in Brandom's philosophy of language is inference. What distinguishes our doings from those of 'non-concept-using creatures' is the inferential articulation in our uses of concepts. Following the title of one of his books, Brandom's expressivism is therefore focused on making things explicit, that is, on making them available for inferences. This programme is distinct from that of *Romantic Expressivism* because Brandom focuses on what is distinctive to the conceptual whereas the Romantics assimilate the conceptual to the linguistic. The conceptual is not equated with the linguistic; it has specific features and specific roles in reasoning.

Despite these differences, he considers pragmatism (and hence his form of *Pragmatic Expressivism*) to share some important features with the Romantics:

> Knowledge is seen rather as an aspect of agency, a kind of doing. Making, not finding, is the genus of human involvement with the world. They share a suspicion of laws, formulae, and deduction. Abstract principle is hollow unless rooted in and expressive of concrete practice. Reality is revealed in the first instance by lived experience, in the life world. Scientific practice and the theories it produces cannot be understood apart from their relation to their

> origin in the skillful attunements of everyday life. Pragmatists and romantics accordingly agree in rejecting universality as a hallmark of understanding. Essential features of our basic, local, temporary, contextualized cognitive engagements with things are leached out in their occasional universalized products. Both see necessity as exceptional, and as intelligible only against the background of the massive contingency of human life. (Brandom 2011, 41)

Both for Romantics and for pragmatists, knowledge is a form of doing rather than an object (*knowing how* rather than *knowing that*). Knowledge is rooted in a specific context or, using a Wittgensteinian vocabulary, a form of life. An important difference remains, however, and it concerns the relation to reason. While both agree on rooting their views of language in the activities and practices in which we use language, they bring this form of pragmatism and its rejection of abstraction in different directions. The Romantics translate this rejection of abstraction as a rejection of reason altogether, thus moving towards a 'literary absolute', while Brandom argues that these practices are precisely central in a game of giving reasons. With this focus on reason, his rationalist pragmatism moves away from the Romantic suspicion against rationality.

The relation between *Pragmatic Expressivism* and *Romantic Expressivism* can be further conceptualized through the lamp metaphor. Indeed, as we have seen, the Romantics suggest considering language as a lamp rather than a mirror, that is, a producer of 'reality' rather than its reflection. Pursuing this metaphorical line, Price suggests another metaphor, that of the projector:

> But if language is not a telescope, then what is it? As Brandom points out, a traditional expressivist option is the lamp. I think that modern technology allows us to make this a little more precise. Think of a data projector, projecting internal images onto an external screen. Even better, helping ourselves to one of tomorrow's metaphors, think of a holographic data projector, projecting three-dimensional images in thin air. This isn't projection *onto* an external, unembellished world. On the contrary, the entire image is free-standing, being simply the sum of all we take to be the case: a world of states of affairs, in all the ways that we take states of affairs to be. (Price 2011, 28)

While he does not refer explicitly to the Romantics – and here is an important difference between Brandom and Price: the former inscribes his philosophy in a historical tradition, the latter does not – Price considers language not as a telescope or a mirror, that is, language as showing us the world better, but as a projector, thus actualizing the Romantic metaphor of language as lamp. More than a lamp that would highlight (and also shadow) aspects of the world, Price suggests seeing language as a holographic data projector: language shapes the world without requiring a background onto which to project it (as a lamp or even a traditional projector would). There is no world to mirror, to look at through a telescope, to enlighten with a lamp or even to project onto with a projector: the projection is the world. With this metaphor, Price pushes the expressivist project (that of the Romantics, but also Brandom's) a step further, and perhaps a step closer to Nietzsche (at least in some interpretations of Nietzsche).

Elsewhere, Price suggests a different metaphor to conceptualize language, one that adds emphasis on the speaker and not just on the world created. The holographic data projector needs no operator, no user; it is a kind of autonomous and self-creating world. To amend this picture, Price considers language as a key.

> My project turns on a contrast between the view of informational content as a passive, 'reflective' sampling of something 'external' and that of it as an active product of an inferential and conversational game – a game whose distinct applications are distinguished by variation at two ends: in the *users*, as well as in the *world*. I'm thus proposing that we abandon the passive conception of representational content in favour of a more active, relational metaphor: that of the *key*, which is adapted at one end to the shape of the user, at the other end to the shape of some part of the environment. (Price 2013, 52)

Against the metaphor of language as a mirror, that is, a passive conception of language representing the world, Price suggests the metaphor of the key, which is adapted both to the user and to the world. A key is a way for a user to open the world and interact with it. There is a mutual shaping that occurs between the user and the world. But, unlike the holographic data projector metaphor, the key metaphor might also suggest that the right key opens the door to somewhere behind the world, a kind of metaphysical 'true world' that Nietzsche criticizes. The problem is that there is no perfect metaphor to express what language does, but we need these metaphors to approach something that cannot be said in other terms. Here the expressive dimension of language is brought to the fore in the very terms of its conceptualization:

metaphors are needed because sometimes description is not enough. Combining the metaphors of the holographic data projector and of the key, we can understand that language is not only a way of shaping the world but also a way of interacting with it. The shaping of the world has always an interaction in view; it has an aim, and a pragmatic one at that. It is this focus on using that shifts from *Romantic Expressivism* to *Pragmatic Expressivism*.

2 Towards a *Pragmatic Expressivism*

One of the main features of *Pragmatic Expressivism* lies in its attempt to reconcile two different strands in conceptualizing language: semantics and pragmatics, thus offering an intersubjective middle ground between the objectivity of a rationalist conception of language and the subjectivity of the Romantics. Usually, semanticists and pragmatists follow different paths, the former towards ideal language philosophy and the latter towards Ordinary Language Philosophy, to use the two forms of philosophy of language that Rorty describes in *The Linguistic Turn*. In his conception of an 'analytic pragmatism', Brandom aims to combine these two paths by showing that pragmatics lies at the heart of semantics (Brandom 2011, 158–9). He conceptualizes the 'meaning as use' pragmatist's theory within an analytic framework by showing what he calls PV and VP relations between vocabularies (V) and practices (P), between semantics and pragmatics.

There are different ways in which PV and VP relations can arise, but Brandom's main idea is to show how some practices rely on certain vocabularies on the one hand and how some vocabularies require certain practices to be deployed on the other:

> I suggested that a way to extend the classical project of semantic analysis so as to take account of the insights of its pragmatist critics is to look analytically at relations between meaning and use. More specifically, I suggested focusing to begin with on two in some sense complementary relations: the one that holds when some set of practices-or-abilities is PV-sufficient to deploy a given vocabulary, and the one that holds when some vocabulary is VP-sufficient to specify a given set of practices-or-abilities. The composition of these is the simplest pragmatically mediated semantic relation between vocabularies: the relation that holds when one

vocabulary is a sufficient pragmatic metavocabulary for another. (Brandom 2008, 24)

Brandom aims to show that the pragmatist conception of meaning as use can be analysed from the perspective of a vocabulary, that is, semantics. Some set of practices can be said to deploy a vocabulary, and a vocabulary can in turn specify a set of practices. It is never one *or* the other, practice *or* vocabulary, pragmatics *or* semantics, but one mediated through the other. This mediation is how Brandom extends the project of semantic analysis that is at the heart of the original project of analytic philosophy (understood here as the Frege-Russell-*Tractatus* conception of language). While pragmatists are considered to take a completely different path, Brandom argues that it is possible to unite them in his analytic pragmatism (thus making the Hegelian move of *aufhebung* between semantics and pragmatics).

Rather than seeing pragmatism as an alternative to the classical project of analysis, Brandom argues that it had always been there in analysis:

> If that is right, then supplementing the traditional philosophical analytical concern with relations between the meanings expressed by different kinds of vocabulary by worrying also about the relations between those meanings and the use of those vocabularies in virtue of which they express those meanings – as I recommended in my first lecture – is not so much extending the classical project of analysis as it is unpacking it, to reveal a pragmatic structure that turns out already to have been implicit in the semantic project all along. For the conclusion I have been arguing for is that it is because some vocabularies are universal pragmatically elaborated and explicitating vocabularies that semantic analysis in the twentieth-century logicist sense is a coherent enterprise at all. (Brandom 2008, 55)

More than extending a project, Brandom is unpacking it, showing that a pragmatic structure lies at the heart of the project of analysis. Brandom therefore characterizes the 'meaning as use' conception as semantics mediated by practice and aims to show that pragmatics plays a central role in language analysis. This pragmatic mediation reveals that, as Glock argues, 'with respect to the analytic/continental divide, pragmatism occupies an ambivalent role' (Glock 2008, 84). Pragmatism is indeed linked to analytic philosophy but also distinct from it and sometimes even presents 'clear affinities with continental philosophy' (Glock 2008, 84). In this respect and as we have seen in Chapter 1, pragmatism would offer a kind of middle ground between analytic and continental, as if the set of pragmatic thinkers could belong to one or another camp, thus blurring the frontier (and perhaps overcoming it).

However, where Brandom's project clearly opposes that of analysis is in the rejection of representationalism. According to Price, this rejection of representationalism is not just offering an alternative theory but, rather, playing a different game. While the game of representationalism can be compared to a matching game in which stickers must match reality, expressivism suggests focusing on the stickers themselves:

> My recommendation is that we deal with this problem by *playing a different game*. In place of the old project of matching stickers to shapes in the natural world, I recommend the project of explaining (in naturalistic terms) how stickers *obtain* their characteristic shapes. Freed of the requirement that they must bear semantic relations to the natural world, stickers – or representations in the systemic, in-game sense – can now occupy a new dimension of their own in the model, orthogonal to the natural world. (Price 2013, 42)

Price therefore focuses on how stickers become stickers, how statements become statements. These stickers do not need to be related to the natural world in a representational way. Rather than being parallel to the world (mirroring it as it were) they are now orthogonal: they operate in a different space.

One of the specificities of Price's expressivism is that it is a global expressivism and not just a local one. While most expressivists consider expressivism to operate locally, Price extends his expressivism to a global dimension.

> The general advantage of this pragmatic direction of explanation is that it is easier to account for the distinctive practical role of the concepts in question – e.g., moral or probabilistic concepts – if we *begin* with that role, than if we begin elsewhere and try to work our way to the use. Once again, traditional expressivists saw this advantage locally. My project seeks to institute it globally. My aim is thus to have all the advantages of traditional expressivism, without the big disadvantage: the need to make good the bifurcation thesis – to find a radical divide in language, where usage marks none. (Price 2013, 41)

With his global expressivism, Price follows a Wittgensteinian view by rejecting the idea that there is an absolute nature in which to ground our discourse.

The problem is that without an absolute in which to ground our practices, we might fall in an 'anything goes' form of relativism.

In reference to Rorty, Blackburn argues that we can avoid this extreme form of relativism by calling on norms. Our discourse is still ruled by norms, and this ruling avoids relativism. However, Blackburn further argues, Rorty's appeal to norms can be problematic:

> It is worth thinking about this a little more carefully. At first sight there seem to be two very different 'norms': one of answerability to the facts, and the different one of gaining unison or solidarity with our fellows. Rorty replies that he sees only one norm, rather than two. He does however admit some content to the cautionary or 'fallibilist' thought that current practice might tell us to affirm that X happened, although the facts may be otherwise. But he glosses the distinction as that between two answers to the question 'To whom are we trying to justify ourselves?' namely 'current practitioners' on the one hand, or 'some other, better informed or more enlightened practitioners' on the other. (Blackburn 2007, 161)

As Blackburn further questions: How can Rorty keep the idea of 'better informed or more enlightened?' Blackburn distinguishes here between normative facts and normative practice. On the one hand, our discourse should meet the facts; on the other, it should meet the practice. In the second case, the practice one, there is no problem with the norm. Within one language-game, one must follow its rules. But the first case, the factual one, raises an important philosophical question: Can we convince someone out of the language-game to come and play it? As long as we remain within practices, pragmatism is very efficient and closes the door to an 'anything goes' relativism. But as soon as we try to move among the practices, it becomes problematic. It must be noted that we can never be outside any practice, we are always playing a game, but we are not all playing the same game. And the question is therefore: Can we convince chess players to come and play football instead? On what grounds can we say football is better than chess? Can we? Appealing to facts will not solve the issue because it brings back representation and its corollary metaphysical 'true world' or absolute grounds.

To solve this problem, Blackburn uses the notion of explanation. Even though we cannot say that our game represents the facts, we can say that in a specific situation, our game provides the most efficient explanation:

> And this, incidentally, solves the problem that bedevilled Cratylus or Nietzsche about the 'adequacy' of words to things. Our words are adequate to things when they represent them as they are, and centrally that requires that what we say best explains our sayings, just as the actual voltage explains the result of a good measurement of the voltage, or a real cliff explains the symbol for a cliff appearing on the map. (Blackburn 2007, 177)

The notion of adequacy is therefore transformed from an ontological one (language mirrors the world) to a pragmatist one (language allows us to do things in the world). Following Price's metaphor, language is not a mirror, but it is a key. Although Blackburn's formulation 'represent them as they are' might suggest a step back towards metaphysics, I think the notion of explanation moves from metaphysics to pragmatics. In Brandom's vocabulary, what makes a representation faithful is that it gives us reasons for action, and it provides a frame for our inferences.

So, what does *Pragmatic Expressivism* leave us with? The rejection of representationalism excludes naturalism and realism in ways of dealing with the world, because there is no world to mirror or represent anymore. However, *Pragmatic Expressivism* avoids an extreme form of relativism by focusing on specific practices (that are ruled by norms). Furthermore, Blackburn argues, this focus on practices shows that realism (but also naturalism, as we will see with Price's subject naturalism) is a form of constructivism after all; that is, it makes up the world rather than reflects it:

> Indeed, [...] it is very difficult indeed to distinguish animation that amounts to real belief, and animation that amounts to immersion in a story that we are prepared to use to predict things and explain things. Our beliefs on the one hand, and the models, fictions, dreams, approximations or metaphors that we employ on the other, may be closer than they seem. (Blackburn 2007, 195)

We cannot go back to an absolute, to 'first philosophy', insofar as it would bring us back in the metaphysical realm which we can never experience (and hence we cannot say anything about it). And we cannot eliminate constructivism insofar as our experience is indistinguishable from a fictional one. What brings us to a real belief or to an immersion in a story is not distinguishable; otherwise, lying would be impossible. If there were a fundamental ontological difference between a real true belief and a fictional one, we could uncover each and every lie. Beliefs and fictions are part of what we employ daily to go on in our everyday life. They are part of our practices, and it is only in our practices (linguistic mainly, but of other sorts as well) that we can interact with and make up the world.

3 The limits of expressivism

As we have seen, *Pragmatic Expressivism* actualizes concerns that occupy not only the pragmatists (including Wittgenstein) but also the Romantic tradition (including Nietzsche). However, the privilege Brandom and others give to reason separates it from *Romantic Expressivism*. This separation brings *Pragmatic Expressivism* away from some insights of Wittgenstein's pluralism and from the capacity of *Romantic Expressivism* to deal with poetic utterances. Indeed, Brandom rejects Wittgenstein's idea that language has no downtown, no centre:

> By contrast to Wittgenstein, the inferential identification of the conceptual claims that language (discursive practice) has a *center*; it is not a motley. Inferential practices of producing and consuming *reasons* are *downtown* in the region of linguistic practice. Suburban linguistic practices utilize and depend on the conceptual contents forged in the game of giving and asking for reasons, are parasitic on it. Claiming, being able to justify one's claims, and using one's claims to justify other claims and actions are not just one among other sets of things one can do with language. They are not on a par with other 'games' one can play. (Brandom 2003, 14–15)

Against the Wittgensteinian idea that there is no privileged language-game, Brandom considers language to have a centre and a rationalist one. Following the urbanistic metaphor, while Wittgenstein does not consider regions of the city to be of different value or importance, just different games to play or places to visit, Brandom affirms that there is a centre and that this centre is more important than other parts of the city. By setting a 'downtown' to language, Brandom must consider other 'games' as parasitical upon the game of claiming and inferring, repeating as it were Austin's (in)famous exclusion of poetic utterances from his consideration (Austin 1975, 22). Although Brandom is not aiming at poetic uses of language per se, affirming the superiority of rational inference over other forms of linguistic connections relegates poetry to a suburb of language.[4] There is, however, little demonstration as to why other practices are of lesser importance. By returning to a rationalist framework (Kantian more than Romantic), Brandom falls back in the difficulties such a framework has with poetic utterances. But what if the centre could move? Isn't it the case for most cities (if we understand by centre the part of the city where life mostly takes place)? What if considering one part as a centre is already a prejudice? Is the centre the same for everyone in a city? I am not saying that poetic utterances are more important and central than claims and inferences, but that they are not less. In discussing Brandom's works, Charles Taylor claims 'that there are certain matters which can't be properly explored without recourse to the disclosive dimension' (Weiss and Wanderer 2010, 35). In other words, as Taylor asks: 'Are our everyday fact-establishing practical games of giving and asking for reasons, which we have shown to be the essential context for all the micro-moves within them, themselves only possible in a broader context, that of the range of symbolic forms which run the full range from pure assertoric to pure disclosive?' (Weiss and Wanderer 2010, 39). The disclosive, including poetic practices, is as instrumental as the assertoric in order to understand language. Poetic practices are of central importance in understanding how creation occurs in language, how language can evolve and adapt. *Pragmatic Expressivism* is primarily rationalist in that making claims and giving and asking for reasons are the downtown of language and thus makes the anti-Wittgensteinian move of attributing a centre to language. However, a similar critique could be addressed to the most extreme forms of *Romantic Expressivism*, the later Heidegger for instance, that place the centre of language in poetry.

While Price follows Brandom in considering that language has a downtown, he argues that this idea does not go against Wittgenstein's understanding of the multiplicity of language-games:

> In my view, however, there's actually no deep conflict here. After all, even Wittgenstein acknowledges the common 'clothing,' which makes different language games superficially similar (and thereby misleads us into thinking that they are all doing the same job). It is open to us to say that the key similarity is precisely that various of the different language games all avail themselves of the same inferential machinery. This is thoroughly compatible with underlying pluralism, so long as we also maintain that the various different kinds of commitments answer to different needs and purposes-

have different origins in our complex natures and relations to our physical and social environments. (Price 2011, 310)

According to Price, Wittgenstein's call on the 'common clothing' of language suggests that there is one form of language that is privileged. This is where I disagree with Price (and Brandom and Blackburn) because the clothing Wittgenstein suggests has nothing to do with a privilege. Wittgenstein's point suggests that as all language-games look alike, that is, they are made of language, we fail to recognize the differences that exist between them. We are (mis)led into considering all language-games as doing the same thing because they superficially look the same. Giving privilege to one language-game is falling into the trap Wittgenstein is warning us against, taking the clothing to be more than mere clothing. Attributing a downtown to language is taking a contingent fact about our uses of language as a necessary essence of all forms of language. Price is making the homogeneity of language a reason to give it a downtown; according to him, 'we shouldn't overlook an important kind of homogeneity within language, comprising the ubiquity and centrality of assertion, of Brandom's "downtown"' (Price 2011, 320). However, by giving centrality to assertion (and leaving aside the disclosive), Price is overlooking the variety of practices, rejecting the pluralism he says he is advocating for, because Wittgenstein's common clothing does not mean that the clothing is the most important (especially because the clothing says nothing except generating confusion between different practices).

To avoid the confusion between different linguistic practices, Brandom follows Rorty in using the term 'vocabulary'. According to Rorty, we use different vocabularies in different situations, and none should be privileged (especially not the vocabulary of representation). If we return to Brandom's discussion of PV and VP relations, we can see how a vocabulary is dependent on a practice (and reciprocally). This talk about vocabulary seems to go against the privilege Brandom gives to the rationalist vocabulary, and that is where Brandom rationalizes Rorty too much (while Rorty remains within the line of Nietzsche and Wittgenstein). However, this notion of vocabulary is interesting to approach poetic phenomena, especially with Rorty's distinction between public and private vocabularies:

Every use of a vocabulary, every application of a concept in making a claim, both is answerable to norms implicit in communal practice – its public dimension, apart from which it cannot mean anything (though it can cause something) – and transforms those norms by its novelty – its private dimension, apart from which it does not formulate a belief, plan, or purpose worth expressing. (Brandom 2011, 153)

Brandom argues that 'Poets and revolutionary scientists break out of their inherited vocabularies to create new ones, as yet undreamed by their fellows' (Brandom 2011, 143). Rorty's notion of vocabulary that Brandom uses here does not only concern the mere choice or range of words but involves a whole culture (vocabulary is related to practice). Rorty develops a distinction between public and private vocabularies: public ones are shared and constitutive of a community (this goes in the sense of Nietzsche's understanding of 'what is common' in BGE) whereas private ones require an initiation and cannot be understood immediately. Rorty argues that 'Every poem, to paraphrase Wittgenstein, presupposes a lot of stage-setting in the culture, for the same reason that every sparkling metaphor requires a lot of stodgy literal talk to serve as its foil' (Rorty 1989, 41). The notion of vocabulary opens a space in language for poetry to occupy. Following this distinction between public and private vocabularies, Brandom argues: 'public discourse corresponding to common purposes, and private discourse to novel purposes. The novel vocabularies forged by artists for private consumption make it possible to frame new purposes and plans that can be appreciated only by those initiated into these vocabularies' (Brandom 2011, 145). Artists and poets – but also philosophers inasmuch as they resemble poets – create new vocabularies which require work from the reader. We could translate this notion of vocabulary in that of style: philosophers – Nietzsche and Wittgenstein are good examples – create new styles in which they can express something different from the common style but which also, in consequence, require work from the reader. The language of the philosopher is no longer to be considered as transparent and immediately accessible but is a use of language which requires interpretation, and therefore active work from the reader. Although this notion of vocabulary is quite insightful, Brandom's insistence on the downtown of language suggests that there is a privileged vocabulary that public vocabularies are first and private ones second. The idea that we need to be initiated to private vocabularies indeed seems to suggest that such vocabularies are not self-explanatory and that they are not autonomous (but in this sense, are we not also initiated to public vocabularies?). What if, however, such private vocabularies were doing the initiation instead? What if they brought us (readers or users) to change and adapt? It is at this point that the talk about vocabularies seems to join Nietzsche's perspectivism.

4 From expressivism to perspectivism

While the departure of *Pragmatic Expressivism* from Wittgenstein's pluralism makes poetic uses of language more problematic, the connection to *Romantic Expressivism* might offer a possibility of bringing poetry back. More specifically, by attempting to reconnect *Pragmatic Expressivism* to its Romantic counterpart, I intend to read *Pragmatic Expressivism* as following a Nietzschean line. This connection in turn also highlights the pragmatic dimension of Nietzsche's philosophy mentioned in Chapter 1. Although a more thorough exploration of Nietzsche's (and Wittgenstein's) 'theories' of language will be the focus of the next chapter, *Pragmatic Expressivism* can be related to Nietzsche. One of the most important connections lies in the revaluation of the notion of truth that is no longer thought of in terms of correspondence insofar as this notion loses all efficiency outside its representational 'home'. The social dimension of linguistic practices no longer grounds truth in an absolute but in the beliefs shared by the practitioners, in what Wittgenstein would call a form of life. These beliefs are further supplemented by desires, and this shift opens the door to a different conception of truth, as Brandom argues:

> For although the pragmatists failed to appreciate the significance of the fact that desires can vary independently of beliefs, they did not simply ignore desires. Rather, they equated the success of actions with the satisfaction of desires, and wanted to attribute to the beliefs that conduced to satisfaction and hence success a special desirable property: their successor notion to the classical concept of truth. (Brandom 2011, 51)

This shift from truth as correspondence (the classical concept of truth) to that of truth as satisfaction of desires (success) can be seen as a Nietzschean move. Truth becomes the force to satisfy desires, and this is one point where Nietzsche fits in a broader picture of philosophy of language, and the notion of force (as well as that of success) is important not only for Nietzsche and the expressivists but also a certain understanding of poetry.[5]

More than a revaluation of truth, the shift Nietzsche operates also marks a shift from truth to use, from essence to action. As Blackburn argues following Nietzsche:

> There is here no equation between utility and truth. On the contrary, the necessary errors and fictions are admittedly useful, but this does not stop Nietzsche from calling them illusions. Here as well we gain a more secure purchase on Nietzsche's association between perspectivism and error. [. . .] In other words, the selection mechanisms that dictate the nature of our perspectives are not there for uncovering the way things are, but for suggesting to us how to act. (Blackburn 2007, 105)

From Nietzsche's perspective, there is no equation between utility and truth because fictions are as useful as truths (if we can even say that there are truths for Nietzsche). In this sense, perspectivism blurs the distinction between fact and fiction. One might argue that, following this line of thought, we end up with no way of distinguishing truth from illusion. Although it is to some extent the case, that is, this Nietzschean line removes all grounds to justify truth, there are still some claims that are patently false (logical contradictions and category mistakes for instance) and other that are purposefully presented as false (or at least hypothetical such as thought experiments for instance).[6] What Nietzsche argues is that such cases are useful insofar as they reveal something of our practices. They are perspectives from which we gain something by experiencing them. In this sense, what perspectivism entails is that our world view becomes a patchwork of perspectives that have proven themselves useful and functional. Moving away from the metaphysical search of 'uncovering the way things are', perspectivism (as a form of pragmatism) suggests to us how to act.

This relation between perspectivism and usefulness connects to a certain conception of functional pluralism that Price develops in his reading of Wittgenstein: '[functional pluralism] plays up the idea that the language concerned has many different functions, in a way that is not evident "on the surface"' (Price 2011, 201). However, if we have a multiplicity of practices with specific aims, how do these relate to the world? It seems that in losing representationalism and the unicity of a grounding principle, we are losing all connection to the world. To address this challenge, Price distinguishes distinction between object and subject naturalism. Indeed, whereas representationalism is often considered a key component of naturalism, Price argues that representationalism is necessary only for object naturalism and not subject naturalism: 'Both the difficulty for the popular view and the conceptual priority of its unpopular rival turn on the foundational role of certain "semantic" or "representationalist" presuppositions in naturalism of the popular sort' (Price 2013, 4). Against object naturalism, Price develops a subject naturalism which, he argues, is inscribed in the line of Nietzsche's naturalism and that allows us to account for nature within the framework of functional pluralism:[7]

> Before we turn to such issues, I want to distinguish object naturalism from a second view of the relevance of science to philosophy. According to this second view, philosophy needs to begin with what science tells us *about ourselves*. Science tells us that we humans are natural creatures, and if the claims and ambitions of philosophy conflict with this view, then philosophy needs to give way. This is naturalism in the sense of Hume, then, and arguably Nietzsche. I'll call it *subject naturalism*. (Price 2013, 5)

Whereas object naturalism tends towards a form of scientism (and hence a line that Nietzsche heavily criticizes), subject naturalism focuses on how science can be of use for existential questions about ourselves and our humanity, while placing a limit to what philosophy can say (the limit being that we are natural creatures, although the definition of 'natural' here remains underdetermined). In this sense, subject naturalism downplays the importance of science or at least restricts its claims: 'Subject naturalism suggests that science might properly take a more modest view of its own importance. It imagines a scientific discovery that science is not all there is – that science is just one thing among many that we do with "representational" discourse' (Price 2013, 21). Science is not all there is; it is one perspective among others, one language-game among others.

In this sense, pluralism *qua* perspectivism undermines the distinction between fact and fiction. Following a Nietzschean interpretation, pluralism replaces facts with perspectives (and hence places the subject as central concern insofar as a perspective is always the perspective of a certain subject).

> The pluralist can thus allow on the one hand that there is no uniform way in which each of the many language-games affects our well-being; and yet on

> the other that in all or most such games there is *some* benefit in argument, and hence in the availability of a notion of truth. In fact, I think the pluralist can do considerably more than this. For it turns out that our use of the notion of truth is *not* strictly uniform across the range of different domains of discourse. There are significant differences, underlying the predominant pattern. I think that pluralism can do much to account for these variations, by appealing to the different functions or linguistic roles of the different domains concerned. And *only* pluralism has the flexibility to do this: other approaches are tied too rigidly to the existence of a fact-stating-non-fact-stating dichotomy in language. (Price 2011, 47)

A pluralist does not need to abandon the notion of truth but, rather, reconsider its scope and application. It is this flexibility (because pluralism relies on the uses of language rather than preconceptions of it) that allows pluralism to account for various language-games, even those in which the question of truth is not related to correspondence. This is because pluralism is no longer tied to the 'fact-stating-non-fact-stating dichotomy in language'. In this context, Price's deflationary approach to truth 'is not only not to be equated with fictionalism, but tends to undermine the fictional-non-fictional distinction, as applied in the metaphysical realm' (Price 2011, 182). While fictionalism still postulates the existence of a metaphysical realm (which can – and must – be fictionalized), expressivism moves away from metaphysics. In this sense, *Pragmatic Expressivism* moves further away from metaphysics than *Romantic Expressivism*, whose conception of truth as disclosure still relies, as we have seen, on the idea that there is something hidden to disclose.

However, what do we do with pluralism? In other words, we have found a multiplicity of practices and no way to distinguish the one we should follow. Have we fallen back into a form of relativism? Where do we go from there? Blackburn argues that perspectivism shows interesting insights to escape relativism. Indeed, the relation usually held between relativism and perspectivism lies on three misconceptions:

> So the metaphor of perspective needs not just one, but three, tonic shots to get us to anything remotely as pessimistic as relativism or scepticism. First, as already described, we would need to jettison one feature of the usual notion: the fact that we can change perspective on things at will, simply by moving around. We would need instead to think that we are trapped in one perspective, and only able to think one way at a time or at best to move our

thoughts very, very slowly. We must imagine our subjectivity in terms of a permanent lens through which we are condemned to take our view of things. Second, we would need the idea that although there are many such different lenses, their results cannot simply be conjoined to give us a comprehensive view that maintains the insights of each. And third, we would need that there is no possible way of ranking them as superior or inferior, in point of truth or accuracy, than one another. And then, if we cling on to the idea of one true way that reality is, we will be drawn to scepticism. And finally, if we discard that idea, leaving only a reality partly created by our perspective, a world-as-it-is-for-us, we will be drawn to Protagorean relativism. (Blackburn 2007, 90)

First, perspectivism is centred around the idea that we can change perspective at will. This might sound like a relativist claim insofar as nothing is fixed, but in fact fixing a perspective is what is relativistic because we would be trapped to thinking relatively to only one perspective, and probably one that is not the best for us. Now Blackburn is perhaps too optimistic in his conception of perspectivism as changing at will, as we will see that for Nietzsche moving through perspectives is not an easy task, although a necessary one. Second, perspectivism would prevent us from reaching any form of 'objectivity'. However, as Nietzsche argues, it is only by moving through perspectives that we can reach a form of 'objectivity', what Wittgenstein calls a 'surveyable representation [*übersichtliche Darstellung*]' (PI 122). Third, perspectivism would mean that all perspectives are equal. This is certainly not the case as the point of perspectivism is precisely to adopt the best perspective possible in view of a specific purpose.

The notion of perspectivism also highlights a point where Blackburn, Brandom and Price disagree. While Price considers expressivism to be global, Blackburn and Brandom adopt a local version of expressivism. The main difference is the scope of application of expressivism: local versions still consider that there are some situations in which representation is needed, while global ones deny this claim. It can, however, be argued that by rooting expressivism in practices (the whole idea of *Pragmatic Expressivism*), the local/global debate is only a superficial one. Blackburn's idea of a 'rolling pragmatism' seems to overcome the distinction and offers an alternative that comes close to perspectivism.

It has been well said that every explanation must start somewhere, but there is no particular place that every explanation has to start. So one could

> imagine a kind of rolling global pragmatism. Whenever an area of discourse becomes a target for philosophical theory and we find ourselves worrying about its ontology or the kind of epistemology or the kind of saying about the world that constitute it, step aside to a place that, at least for the moment, seems not so worrisome and essay a pragmatic story about the utility of the target way of thought and talk, given an environment composed in the other, less demanding way. (Price 2013, 80)

Such a 'rolling pragmatism' would be a sort of perspectivism that would overcome the local/global debate in expressivism. We must begin our investigation somewhere (and this can be anywhere) and move from one perspective to another according to our needs. With this notion of perspectivism, *Pragmatic Expressivism* inherits not only from the later Wittgenstein but also from Nietzsche's philosophy. Blackburn suggests that 'Global pragmatism would be a patchwork of local pragmatisms, living by taking in each other's washing' (Price 2013, 82). In this sense, the debate between globalists and localists does not make sense. In the end, local pragmatism can be extended to a global form insofar as there is no privileged perspective. A local pragmatism that would reject globalization would be a strange mixture between an absolute perspective overarching local ones.

Perspectivism *qua* global pragmatism/expressivism therefore builds the world as a patchwork of perspectives understood in the pragmatic way of actions, doings and interactions. However, this patchwork is not hiding a world underneath; it is the world itself. This idea of patchwork substitutes itself to the metaphysical idea of the world or of 'reality'. Brian Lightbody describes this patchwork as Nietzsche's *quilt* that he opposes to Brandom's *cloak*:

> In conclusion, Brandom compares his theory of sapience, infused as it is by a robust normativity, to be much like an inferential cloak thrown over the nakedness of the world. What's more, once the world is so enveloped, the cloak becomes impossible to cast off and yet there is no denying that something lies underneath it. Nietzsche, in contrast, views normativity as a quilt comprised of patches that are then stitched together and where the underlying thread running through each square – whether it depicts the enwalling of our ancestors, the creation of a system of credits and debts, or the separation of a priestly caste and warrior caste from the human herd – is the will to power. [. . .] Nietzsche's quilt is not thrown over the world such

that it hides a distinct object underneath, but is, as it were, the world balled up. (Lightbody 2020, 647)

According to Lightbody, even though Brandom rejects representationalism, his theory still relies on there being something under the cloak, which would reopen the door to metaphysical investigations. (What is under this cloak? What is the real world behind appearances?) In this sense, Brandom remains in the Kantian framework: there is a noumenal world behind the phenomenal one, but we cannot access it (but our reason justifies its existence). On the contrary, Nietzsche rejects this dualistic picture, and his perspectivism consists of a patchwork of interpretations in which there is no ultimate one and under which there is nothing. Nietzsche's perspectivism joins Blackburn's 'rolling pragmatism' in offering a global expressivism retaining some possibilities for local representational features (in specific language-games). Against the rationalism of *Pragmatic Expressivism*, Nietzsche appears as a 'power-pragmatist' (Lightbody 2020, 647) whose perspectivism overcomes the debate between local and global expressivism. In this sense, Nietzsche's perspectivism (and we will see that Wittgenstein can be interpreted as holding a similar view) sits as a middle ground between *Romantic Expressivism* and *Pragmatic Expressivism*, a middle ground in which neither rationality nor subjectivity is given a privileged position in relating to the world.

4

From Wittgenstein to Nietzsche and back

> *This has given me the greatest trouble and still does: to realize that what things are called is incomparably more important than what they are.*
> Nietzsche, *The Gay Science*, §58

In the previous chapters, I have been arguing that expressivism is the best direction to follow in order to elaborate a philosophy of language that can account for poetic phenomena. However, we have seen that both *Romantic Expressivism* and *Pragmatic Expressivism* have their limits: the former retains a metaphysical dimension by sacralizing the disclosive whereas the latter operates the traditional move of considering poetic uses of language as secondary. My aim is therefore to find a middle ground between these two forms of expressivism, and I argue that it lies at the intersection of Nietzsche's and Wittgenstein's views on language, insofar as the former inherits from the Romantic tradition but moves towards a broader understanding of language and as the latter is the point of origin of contemporary developments of *Pragmatic Expressivism*. Connecting Nietzsche and Wittgenstein opens a path towards a philosophy of language that encompasses poetry and that bridges across the analytic–continental divide.

If, as I have argued, the so-called analytic–continental divide is only a misrepresentation insofar as neither side can be adequately defined, it should not be an obstacle to connecting Nietzsche and Wittgenstein. Quite to the contrary as the confrontation of these two philosophers – as the confrontation between philosophers supposedly belonging to one and the other tradition usually does – opens new paths of reflection. Such a confrontation is particularly germane in aesthetics, as philosophy in this field seems to still conform to the misrepresentation of the divide.[1] Insofar as poetry is essentially a linguistic matter, it is necessary to explore Nietzsche's and Wittgenstein's views on language before turning to aesthetic concerns in the philosophy of poetry. As already seen in Chapter 2, Nietzsche and Wittgenstein both inherit from a similar tradition which rejects representationalism and explores the possibilities of expressivism, which Charles Taylor calls the 'HHH view' and that is rooted in eighteenth-century German philosophy of language. Although the direct connections between Nietzsche and Wittgenstein are scarce – we know Wittgenstein has read some of Nietzsche's works but it is difficult to say what he thought of him – the expressive tradition of language represents an important common ground through which Nietzsche and Wittgenstein share similar concerns regarding the end of metaphysics and the role language plays in it.

Before looking at their views on language, we must keep in mind that they do not elaborate a *philosophy of language* in the sense of a clearly exposed theory but, as their aphoristic style suggests, only present ideas on language which never amount to a system.[2] Any attempt to systematize their thoughts misses the performative character of their writing and can thus be misleading. I therefore do not aim to uncover a theory of language in their writings, but rather to show how their philosophical gesture share some similarities that can help us considering poetic phenomena within an expressivist framework, thus building a form of *Poetic Expressivism*. This similarity in gesture can be found in the idea that philosophy is a therapeutic activity, that philosophy should not be thought in terms of product but in terms of process. As a therapeutic process, philosophy becomes a transformative experience for Nietzsche and Wittgenstein, as Glen Martin argues that 'both are ultimately looking, or hoping, for a transformation of human existence which will lead us out of the suicidal problems in which the modern world is entangled' (Martin 1989, 2). This existential dimension of Nietzsche's and Wittgenstein's philosophies turns to an auto-reflexive dimension in which philosophy is aware of its own presentation that connects philosophy to poetry.[3] To put it in another way, as Ray Monk suggests: 'Wittgenstein's lecturing style, and indeed his writing style, was curiously at odds with its subject-matter, as though a poet had somehow strayed into the analysis of the foundations of mathematics and the Theory of Meaning' (Monk 1991, 291). The first step towards such a transformation of philosophy is to operate a critique of traditional philosophy as metaphysics. It is in this sense that Alain Badiou considers Nietzsche and Wittgenstein to both be 'antiphilosophers' who criticize metaphysics and traditional views on language. In this sense, they are both 'Sprachkritker' *à la* of Fritz Mauthner as mentioned in Chapter 1. Janet Lungstrum insists on this connection through Mauthner but considers them to, however, differ in their relation to rules: while Nietzsche seeks 'a cyclical *destruction* and *re-creation* of the rules [whereas] Wittgenstein's program is to survey theoretical possibilities of the twists and turns of the already sayable by an ostensibly less ambitious, new "Ordnen" of "was schon offen zutage liegt"' (Lungstrum 1995, 318–19).

There are three parts to this chapter. In the first, I focus on relating the linguistic turn to the end of metaphysics in order to inscribe Nietzsche and Wittgenstein in this shared context. This will lead me, in the second part, to consider Wittgenstein's critique of metaphysical language and to show how these aspects relate to some of Nietzsche's views on language mentioned in Chapter 1. The critique of metaphysics, however, leaves philosophy and language without a grounding that can lead to relativism, as mentioned in the previous chapters. In the last section, I therefore untangle the charge of relativism and show that Nietzsche and Wittgenstein both offer a way to escape nihilism and scepticism through a reconsideration of language.

1 The linguistic turn and the end of metaphysics

The opening quotation from Nietzsche's GS suggests a shift from 'what things are' to 'what things are called' that prefigures in some ways the 'linguistic turn' of twentieth-century philosophy. This shift to language originates in the critique of metaphysics understood as the search for the essence of things, as the positing of a true world beyond the apparent one. For Nietzsche, this shift away from metaphysics entails an increased attention to history: it is a shift from considering things as determinate – having an essence – to considering them as ever-changing – having a history. Nietzsche suggests such a shift as one from metaphysical to historical philosophy in the opening sections of HH: 'But everything has become: there are *no eternal facts*, just as there are no absolute truths. Consequently what is needed from now on is *historical philosophizing*, and with it the virtue of modesty' (HH 2 / KSA 2.25, emphasis in original). More than that, Nietzsche considers that the changes are embedded in how things are called, in their names. A name is not only a signifier but also bears many prejudices and evaluations which evolve through time. The turn to language is one way to oppose the project of metaphysics, and Nietzsche takes this turn from the perspective of history (or genealogy in the later works): as meanings evolve through time and as this evolution must be taken into account as belonging to the meaning of the words, there can be no absolute, context-independent meaning. Wittgenstein's conception of 'meaning as use' suggests a similar idea: there is no 'meaning' outside of the use we make of the words, and this use is, for Nietzsche, defined historically and contextually. In this sense, meaning is made rather than found, and this making connects to the task of poetry in its etymological sense of *poiesis*.

As we have seen in the previous chapters, with the end of metaphysics must come the end of a metaphysical conception of language which suggests that 'through [words and concepts] we are grasping the *essence* of things' (WS 11 / KSA 2.547). Such metaphysical conceptions of language are 'magic' in the sense that they see language as self-interpreting, as Samuel Wheeler suggests. A metaphysical conception of language considers the meaning of words to be unequivocal and explained through the relation between word and world. A critique of representationalism is a critique of metaphysics, insofar as it criticizes the foundations on which metaphysics is built. As already mentioned in Chapter 3, representationalism can be compared to a child's matching game as Huw Price suggests: 'Matching true statements to the world seems a lot like matching stickers to the picture; and many problems in philosophy seem much like the problems the child faces when some of the stickers are hard to place' (Price 2013, 23). One domain in which 'stickers' are especially hard to place is poetry, and one of the main problems of a representationalism is its failure to account for literary or metaphorical statements: such statements are either patently false, the sticker does not match the picture like in Magritte's famous 'ceci n'est pas une pipe', or meaningless because they refer to nothing.

Nietzsche and the later Wittgenstein reject representationalism and ground their critique of metaphysics in this rejection. They inherit from the 'HHH view' which defends an 'expressive' conception of language which, as Taylor puts it, 'shows us language as the locus of different kinds of disclosure. It makes us aware of the expressive dimension and its importance. And it allows us to identify a constitutive dimension, a way in which language does not only represent, but enters into some of the realities it is "about"' (Taylor 1985, 273). Expressivism cannot take truth to be a matter of correspondence because language no longer only mirrors the world but also takes part in shaping it.[4] Truth therefore becomes a matter of disclosure: a statement is considered true not if it matches some kind of 'reality' but if it reveals or discloses something of the world. In other words, a true expressive statement must not necessarily correspond to a fact but, rather, reveal something which will enrich one's understanding.[5] We must, however, be wary of this idea of disclosure as it seems to bring metaphysics back into the picture, as if there were a true world behind the apparent one. I will argue in the next chapters that we can understand disclosive truth in terms of significance: such truths reveal how things make sense for us and how they become significant.

The opposition between expressive and representational conceptions of language – like the common view on the analytic–continental divide described in Chapter 1 – can be translated in terms of the opposition between art and science. As Tzvetan Todorov argues, while describing what happens within literature with the Romantics:

> Art and poetry relate to a truth that is not of the same nature as the truth towards which science aspires. [. . .] Science states propositions which are said to be true or false when confronted to the facts they describe. [. . .] It is a *truth of correspondence*. To the contrary, when Baudelaire says that 'The Poet is like the prince of the clouds,' i.e., the albatross, this claim cannot be verified. However, Baudelaire does not talk nonsense: he aims at disclosing the poet's identity. In this context, he aspires to a *truth of disclosure*, he attempts to reveal the nature of a being, a situation, a world. In both cases, a relation is established between words and world, but the two kinds of truth remain distinct. [. . .] To conclude we can say that art does not only lead a knowledge of the world, but that it also reveals the existence of this truth of a different nature. In reality, this truth does not belong exclusively to art as it constitutes the horizon of other interpretative discourses: history, human sciences, philosophy.[6] (Todorov 2007, 59–61)

According to Todorov, truth as correspondence would be the tool of science, whereas truth as disclosure would belong to the realms of poetry and the other arts. These truths are each linked to a specific conception of language, representational or expressive, and these conceptions of language could therefore be classified in the same way: representational conceptions of language belong to the realm of science and expressive ones to that of art. These distinctions should, however, not be considered as definite but only indicate a general direction. It is important to note that, for Todorov at least, one truth is not better than the other: both say something of the world and are therefore important. What is at play is that language should no longer be considered as mirroring a metaphysically posited 'reality' but as shaping the world we live in.

2 Wittgenstein and the traps of language

Wittgenstein shares Nietzsche's suspicion of metaphysical uses of language: philosophy is an activity, a therapy, that aims to cure and free us from the traps of language. Close to the end of the *Tractatus*, he argues that philosophy has essentially a negative task, that of showing the meaninglessness of metaphysical propositions:

> The correct method in philosophy would really be the following: to say nothing except what can be said, i.e. propositions of natural science – i.e. something that has nothing to do with philosophy – and then, whenever someone else wanted to say something metaphysical, to demonstrate to him that he had failed to give a meaning to certain signs in his propositions. Although it would not be satisfying to the other person – he would not have the feeling that we were teaching him philosophy – this method would be the only strictly correct one. (T 6.53)

Wittgenstein insists that this negative method would be the only correct one, and philosophy would therefore have nothing more to construct. In Wittgenstein's later works, the critique of metaphysics shifts because his conception of language has a radically different scope from that of the *Tractatus*. Whereas the *Tractatus* focuses on 'ideal' language, and thereby remains within the framework of representationalism, the later works focus on 'ordinary' language. The critique remains, metaphysical language must be avoided, but, rather than being kept silent, metaphysical statements should be brought back to their ordinary use. Wittgenstein's *Tractatus* remains trapped into the metaphysics of language, and its critique of metaphysics therefore fails. In that sense, the later Wittgenstein is much closer to Nietzsche's views seen in Chapter 1:

> When philosophers use a word – 'knowledge,' 'being,' 'object,' 'I,' 'proposition/ sentence,' 'name' – and try to grasp the *essence* of the thing, one must always

ask oneself: is the word ever actually used in this way in the language in which it is at home? –

What *we* do is to bring words back from their metaphysical to their everyday use. (PI 116)

The problem with the philosophers' use of language is that they believe words to refer to metaphysical entities. For instance, when they use the word 'being', they do not use it in its ordinary way, which causes no problem, but in a metaphysical one, as if by using the word 'being' they were getting to the essence of the thing. Wittgenstein's point is not to reduce language to something simpler – that is what he has done in the *Tractatus*, reducing language to logic and placing boundaries to what can be said – but to avoid making it anything more than it is. Metaphysical uses of language push words out of their ordinary use and take them as directly linked to some kind of essence.

As we have seen in Chapter 1, metaphysical uses of language are captive of the picture of representationalism. This metaphysical picture – language gives us a direct relation to the nature of things – is what leads us to many philosophical confusions. This is also why Wittgenstein criticizes Augustine's picture of language in the opening sections of PI: 'These words, it seems to me, give us a particular picture of the essence of human language. It is this: the words in language name objects – sentences are combinations of such names' (PI 1). Augustine's picture of language and the one Wittgenstein elaborates in the *Tractatus* are similar in the sense that they trap us into a metaphysical conception of language. However, this picture of language belongs to our language, and that is why it is so difficult to get away from it. Wittgenstein's aim to bring the word back from their metaphysical to their ordinary use is an attempt at getting out of this trap. In his later works, his aim is therefore not to elaborate an ideal language but to describe the ordinary one: 'The task of philosophy is not to create an ideal language, but to clarify the use of existing language' (PG 72).

The picture, the trap, that held us captive is the idea that language is fundamentally representational, and that it can be reduced to an ideal form. In contrast, Wittgenstein insists on our linguistic practices that he calls 'language-games':

We can also think of the whole process of using words in (2) as one of those games by means of which children learn their native language. I will

> call these games '*language-games*' and will sometimes speak of a primitive language as a language-game.
>
> And the processes of naming the stones and of repeating words after someone might also be called language-games. Think of certain uses that are made of words in games like ring-a-ring-a-roses.
>
> I shall also call the whole, consisting of language and the activities into which it is woven, a 'language-game.' (PI 7)

The Augustinian picture of language in which words name things and the meaning of a word is its reference is therefore only one language-game among many others. It is not an adequate description of our whole language because there is no such thing as *the* language. On the contrary, the notion of language-games brings into focus the fact that there are various linguistic practices: each language-game brings light on one or another aspect of language, on one or another practice. Interestingly, a primitive form of representational language reveals that the meaning of a word is not its reference (at least not in all language-games) but is its use within the game: 'So, one could say: an ostensive definition explains the use – the meaning – of a word if the role the word is supposed to play in the language is already clear' (PI 30). The meaning of a word is its use in a language-game, and an ostensive definition can explain the meaning of a word only if the use of the word is already known. In other words, an ostensive definition does not work as a primitive explanation as it presupposes that one already knows how a word can be used.

The main problem Wittgenstein sees in the metaphysical use of language is therefore its 'craving for generality' and its blindness to the multiplicity of uses. Inasmuch as Nietzsche criticizes the 'equating of unequal things' through the use of concepts, Wittgenstein sees in concepts a tendency towards generalization which causes philosophical error and confusion: 'This craving for generality is the resultant of a number of tendencies connected with particular confusion' (BB, p. 17). Importantly, one of these tendencies is 'our preoccupation with the method of science' and the reduction necessary for it to operate. 'This tendency is the real source of metaphysics and leads the philosopher into complete darkness' (BB, p. 18). Like Nietzsche and his critique of scientism, Wittgenstein does not follow science blindly. The task of philosophy is not to follow the 'method of science' and reduce language to what it is not: 'it can never be our job to reduce anything to anything, or to explain anything. Philosophy really *is* "purely descriptive"' (BB, p. 18). In PI, Wittgenstein pursues this thought: 'Philosophy must not interfere in any way with the actual use of language, so it can in the end only describe it. For it cannot justify it either. It leaves everything as it is' (PI 124). The task of philosophy is not to modify language (or reduce it to a logical, ideal one) but to look at, describe and understand ordinary language (and through language, our relation to and conception of the world). It might seem that Wittgenstein's insistence on description leaves little space for change in language and that it would therefore be ill-suited to account for poetic uses of language. However, as we have seen in Chapter 3, Wittgenstein is more a constructivist than a quietist in this regard, and we will see that his insistence on inventing new language-games is instrumental in approaching poetry in the next chapters.

Wittgenstein's critique of the philosophical craving for generality is a critique of metaphysics on the grounds of one of its key presuppositions, namely the existence of definite concepts. As Michael Forster argues, this critique goes against the presuppositions of Plato's metaphysics and many of his followers: 'One fundamental point which he is concerned to establish with his demonstration of the family resemblance character of many concepts is that a certain theory about the nature of all general concepts that was first propounded by Plato, and then taken over by Aristotle, and by many philosophers since even down to the present day, is mistaken' (Forster 2010, 71). As we have seen, Nietzsche also criticizes Plato and considers him to be the first event in the history of metaphysics in TI. He even states in an early note that 'My philosophy is an inverted Platonism: the further something is from true being, the purer, the more beautiful, the better it is. Living in illusion as the goal' (NF 1870-1871, 7[156] / KSA 7.199). Even though Nietzsche's inversion of Platonism is to be understood in the perspective of his critique of the metaphysical dualism between true and apparent worlds, Nietzsche's and Wittgenstein's critiques are not unrelated. Plato's metaphysics (and the dualism it entails) relies on a metaphysical conception of language. By criticizing Plato's conception of the nature of concepts underlying the whole tradition of metaphysics, Wittgenstein works in the same direction as Nietzsche because the metaphysical dualisms cannot stand without concepts having a definite nature.

If concepts no longer have a definite nature, can they still be called concepts? How do they function? It is to answer these questions that Wittgenstein elaborates a specific kind of concept that he calls 'family resemblance' concepts and that will prove very useful to approach 'open' concepts such as art and poetry. As he develops this idea, there are some affinities and similarities between various linguistic practices. Against the idea of a language with a definite essence, Wittgenstein considers language to be made of various language-games that have different affinities. He takes the example of 'games' to illustrate this: 'For if you look at [games], you won't see something that is common to *all*, but similarities, affinities, and a whole series of them at that. To repeat: don't think, but look!' (PI 66). When we look at different games – and Wittgenstein insists on *looking at* rather than thinking about, the point is to observe and describe – we cannot find a single element common to all games, but we can find a 'whole series of similarities and affinities'. Rather than thinking about a common essence to classify games under the label 'games', Wittgenstein looks at similarities and affinities between what is usually called 'games'. This means that the cluster of things united under the label 'games' is not closed and can be expanded, but, correlatively, it cannot be given sharp boundaries: 'And the upshot of these considerations is: we see a complicated network of similarities overlapping and criss-crossing: similarities in the large and in the small' (PI 66). Rather than establishing and defining a concept, Wittgenstein shows the network of affinities and similarities in a family. Against the rigidity of the metaphysical notions of category and concept, Wittgenstein develops the notion of family resemblance which can render the ever-changing and evolving character of language.

Quite surprisingly, and even though Nietzsche does not theorize this notion of concepts as family resemblance, he uses this exact term in BGE:

> That individual philosophical concepts are not something isolated, something unto themselves, but rather grow up in reference and relatedness to one another; that however suddenly and arbitrarily they seem to emerge in the history of thought, they are as much a part of one system as the branches of fauna on one continent: this is revealed not least by the way the most disparate philosophers invariably fill out one particular schema of *possible* philosophies. [. . .] This easily explains the strange family resemblance (*Familien-Ähnlichkeit*) of all Indian, Greek, and German philosophizing. Wherever linguistic affinity, above all, is present, everything necessary for an analogous development and sequence of philosophical systems will inevitably be on hand from the beginning, thanks to the shared

philosophy of grammar (I mean thanks to being unconsciously ruled and guided by similar grammatical functions), just as the way to certain other possibilities for interpreting the world will seem to be blocked. Philosophers from the Ural-Altaic linguistic zone (where the concept of the subject is less developed) will most probably look differently 'into the world' and will be found on other paths than Indo-Germans or Muslims: and in the last analysis, the spell of certain grammatical functions is the spell of *physiological* value judgements and conditions of race.

This by way of a rejection of Locke's superficiality concerning the origins of ideas. (BGE 20 / KSA 5.34-5)

This paragraph contains quite a few themes and ideas that we can also find in Wittgenstein's later works. Nietzsche considers that philosophical concepts share a resemblance, and that the family resemblance of various types of philosophizing shows they share something in common. Philosophy is, according to Nietzsche, a family resemblance concept because it is strongly tied to a language: philosophies in the same language will share affinities. Philosophy is, however, not the only domain developed in language; we have seen that science, religion and morality are all dependent on language. Nietzsche does not specify whether other concepts are family resemblance concepts as well, but we are strongly inclined to believe that concepts such as science, religion and morality are. We could read the transformation process from metaphor to concept as putting together things that have a family resemblance with each other. However, Nietzsche does not develop his thoughts further on that matter, and 'family resemblance' only appears this one time in all his works. This notion, however, suggests that Nietzsche considers concepts to be relative to a language or culture, in a way similar to Wittgenstein's 'form of life'. Concepts belong to a particular language and form a culture, a world view. Moreover, the way things are seen depends on the concepts or words one has at one's disposal. In that sense, Nietzsche's remarks concerning the development of the concept of subject in the Ural-Altaic linguistic zone leads to a form of relativism close to that of Sapir-Whorf: the world view depends on the concepts one has. In a perspectival vocabulary, the world depends on the optics through which it is seen, and Wittgenstein's notion of 'form of life' could be interpreted as playing a similar role: the 'form of life' or culture we live in affects the way we see the world. Nietzsche and Wittgenstein share the critique of definite concepts (and Nietzsche in a way more radical than Wittgenstein), but they do not offer the same solution. Nietzsche rejects rigid concepts and tries to go back to metaphor, to the uniqueness of each experience (even though he acknowledges the necessity of fixation in language for community to exist) whereas Wittgenstein develops the notion of family resemblance concepts in order to group similar things under one category while allowing some adjusting in their use.

Despite the advantages of family resemblance concepts, especially to give an account of ever-changing domains such as art and poetry, as we will see in the next chapters, the loss of rigidity entails the loss of boundaries and with this loss the risk of relativism. What are the limits of a family resemblance concept? Wittgenstein argues that boundaries are not necessarily closed and that closed boundaries are not necessary to define or explain a word. But if there are no boundaries to a concept, it could encompass anything and be unregulated: there lies the risk of an 'anything goes' relativism. Wittgenstein considers this objection: "'But then the use of the word is unregulated – the 'game' we play with it is unregulated.'' – It is not everywhere bounded by rules; but no more are there any rules for how high one may throw the ball in tennis, or how hard, yet tennis is a game for all that, and has rules too' (PI 68). For Wittgenstein, it is not so much of a problem that the game is unregulated because rules never operate on all aspects of the game. There are some rules which shape the framework for the game, and there is some space for adjusting and interpretation. Whereas definite concepts are somehow dogmatic, deciding what belongs to and what does not, family resemblance concepts call for interpretation, and interpretation can vary according to the interpreter or to time. While this seems at first glance to lead to an 'anything goes' form of relativism, there are rules for interpretation to make sense that restrict the relativism about rules: some aspects are regulated and others are not, depending on the game we play.

3 Relativism, pragmatism, perspectivism

In TI, Nietzsche acknowledges, like Wittgenstein, that we are being held captive by language but suggests that one of the reasons for that is our entrapment within the bounds of rationality:

> Language began at a time when psychology was in its most rudimentary form: we enter into a crudely fetishistic mindset when we call into consciousness the basic presuppositions of the metaphysics of language – in the vernacular: the presuppositions of reason. It sees doers and deeds all over: it believes that will has causal efficacy: it believes in the 'I', in the I as being, in the I as substance, and it projects this belief in the I-substance onto all things – this is how it creates the concept of 'thing' in the first place. (TI 'Reason' 5 / KSA 6.77)

One of the reasons we are trapped in the metaphysics of language is rationality. Reason leads us to project our belief onto things because things must have an explanation. For instance, the belief in the 'I' as substance is precisely what Wittgenstein criticizes in metaphysical uses of language: because philosophers aim at the essence of the 'I', they move away from the ordinary understanding of it, from the practices in which it is embedded. For Nietzsche, the problem is that by doing so, the philosopher eradicates the whole psychology and physiology at play in the human subject, in other words the whole context in which the word occurs, basically that my 'I' is not identical to Descartes's 'I' or Wittgenstein's 'I'; and perhaps even, following Heraclitus's saying that 'No man ever steps in the same river twice', that my 'I' is never self-same, that as Arthur Rimbaud says 'Je est un autre'. The metaphysician's 'I' is an inanimate, abstract and general one, whereas in language the 'I' is always particular.

Metaphysics focuses on substances and general ideas because it isolates things and opposes them: 'The metaphysicians' fundamental belief is *the belief in the opposition of values*' (BGE 2 / KSA 5.16). The important term here is 'belief'. Metaphysical language is based on beliefs (and even reason itself is based on beliefs), and that is one of the reasons Nietzsche turns to psychology as 'the queen of the sciences' (BGE 23 / KSA 5.39). This term of belief leads Nietzsche to compare metaphysics and language to religion: '"Reason" in language: oh, what a deceptive old woman this is! I am afraid that we have not got rid of God because we still have faith in grammar' (TI 'Reason' 5 / KSA 6.78). The beliefs on which metaphysical language relies are the same as those on which religion and morality rely that Nietzsche criticizes at various points in his works. This relation of language to culture is what Wittgenstein expresses through his notion of 'forms of life'. When he says that 'to imagine a language means to imagine a form of life' (PI 19), we could see it in the Nietzschean sense of imagining a range of valuation. Hence, Nietzsche's attempt at a revaluation of all values calls for a revaluation of language: there can be no revolution in values without revolution in language.

With this critique of language and of the prejudices embedded in it, Nietzsche adopts a position close to Wittgenstein and other proponents of the 'linguistic analysis'. Richard Schacht, following Arthur Danto, even considers Nietzsche as both a precursor and critic *avant la lettre* of 'analytic philosophy' understood as linguistic analysis (Schacht 1974, 154). Indeed, they consider that philosophers must free themselves from the charms of language to avoid metaphysical errors. However, and quite importantly, Nietzsche does not follow early analytic philosophy on the path of ideal language philosophy as he denies that logic has the power to solve the problems of metaphysical knowledge. On the contrary, Nietzsche considers logic to be as problematic as language because it is based on the same belief in 'absolute truth'. Whereas the early Wittgenstein and 'linguistic analysis' use logic as an ideal language to solve the problems embedded in natural language, Nietzsche does not believe that logic can be helpful because it is based on the same principles as metaphysical or 'magic' language. Although propositional logic might be (as the belief in truth and language) a condition for life, it is also the basis for the formation of concepts and metaphysical forms: 'Logic is merely slavery in the bonds of language. But language contains an illogical element, such as metaphor etc. The initial force causes unequal things to be equated and is thus an effect of the imagination. This is the foundation of concepts, forms, etc.' (KSA 7:29[8]). If we relate this fragment to TL, logic is the force which fixes metaphors. Nietzsche can compare logic to slavery because he sees logic as enslaving and 'equating unequal things' (*Gleichsetzen des Ungleichen*). Language itself possesses an illogical dimension which is represented by metaphor. This illogical dimension is that presented by poetry and literature for instance as they do not rely on the rules of logic. The value of logical truth must therefore also be put into question. Logical truth is only one kind of truth among others and, according to Nietzsche, not the most prominent or important one.

Nietzsche criticizes logic on the same grounds he criticizes concepts. His focus on metaphor and interpretation entails a revaluation of the conception of knowledge. Such a conception of knowledge has famously been construed as Nietzsche's perspectivism which Danto summarizes in saying 'there are no facts but only interpretations' (Danto 2005, 59). Many commentators consider perspectivism as problematic, and Maudemarie Clark for instance considers that 'Although perspectivism denies metaphysical truth, it is perfectly compatible with the minimal correspondence account of truth and therefore with granting that many human beliefs are true' (Clark 1990, 135). Clark's answer aims at saving Nietzsche from relativism but requires a fine distinction between two theories of truth. As I will argue in the next chapter, the main problem of Clark's account, and the main reason commentators consider perspectivism as problematic, is that she considers perspectivism as a doctrine whereas Nietzsche's texts always attempt to avoid such theorizing and that she remains within the framework of representationalism. Moreover, perspectivism is not necessarily linked to relativism insofar as, Babette Babich argues, relativism is always tied to an ideal (an absolute) the relativist claims we cannot reach, whereas Nietzsche's perspectivism is tied to no absolute at all (Babich 1994, 48). This nuance does, however, not solve the problem of self-contradiction which, as I will argue in the next chapter, can be avoided by relating perspectivism to poetry. Let us note already that Nietzsche does not deny truth itself, but questions the value of truth and the preference for truth over untruth as he argues in the first paragraph of BGE: 'Given that we want truth: *why do we not prefer* untruth? And uncertainty? Even ignorance? The problem of the value of truth appeared before us – or did we before it?' (BGE 1 / KSA 5.15).

Nietzsche's critiques of language and truth occur within his project of revaluation of all values. Nietzsche does not criticize language or truth in themselves (for it would rely on a metaphysical understanding of them and such a criticism would be impossible from within language) but criticizes the value we attribute to them. His critiques of language and truth are to be understood within the larger framework of his critique of culture (and we have seen that his critique of culture and his critique of metaphysics are intimately related). A revaluation of all values means a revaluation of the foundations of our culture. As long as the philosopher (or anyone else) does not put into question her belief in or valuation of language and truth, she remains, borrowing an image from one of Nietzsche's early notes, 'caught in the nets of *language*' (KSA 7:19[135]). These nets of language are a metaphysical trap of which Nietzsche and Wittgenstein make us aware and wary.

Indeed, Wittgenstein also uses this image of language as a trap, for instance, in CV:

> Language sets everyone the same traps; it is an immense network of well kept wrong turnings. And hence we see one person after another walking down the same paths and we know in advance the point at which they will branch off, at which they will walk straight on without noticing the turning, etc., etc. So what I should do is erect signposts at all the junctions where there are wrong turnings, to help people past the danger points. (CV, p. 25)

The philosopher should be a guide in the maze of language. The task of the philosopher is therefore not to clarify language in the sense of making it simpler or idealizing it, but to indicate where dangers or traps can be found in ordinary language. Wittgenstein also compares language to a labyrinth in PI: 'Language is a labyrinth of paths. You approach from *one* side and you know your way about; you approach the same place from another side and no longer know your way about' (PI 203). The task of the philosopher then becomes to discover the traps and to show a way to avoid them or, as Wittgenstein says, 'What is your aim in philosophy? – To show the fly the way out of the fly-bottle' (PI 309). Nietzsche's solution involves the ideas of perspectivism and interpretation (which brings the perceiving subject to the fore, against Descartes' primacy of the thinking I) whereas Wittgenstein replaces the metaphysical conception of 'language' with a more pragmatic multiplicity of 'language-games' which he grounds in the notion of 'form of life'.

This context in which language occurs, this form of life, is something cultural which could be interpreted in Nietzschean terms as the value judgements or the map of values with which this game operates. Our language depends on our culture and to imagine a language is to imagine a culture in which this language can make sense:

> Imagine a use of language (a culture) in which there was a common name for green and red on the one hand and yellow and blue on the other. Suppose, e.g., that there were two castes, one the patrician caste, wearing red and green garments the other, the plebeian, wearing blue and yellow garments. Both yellow and blue would always be referred to as plebeian colours, green and red as patrician colours. Asked what a red patch and a green patch have in common, a man of our tribe would not hesitate to say they were both patrician.
>
> We could also easily imagine a language (and that means again a culture) in which there existed no common expression for light blue and dark blue, in

which the former, say, was called 'Cambridge', the latter 'Oxford'. If you ask a man of this tribe what Cambridge and Oxford have in common, he'd be inclined to say 'Nothing'. (BB, pp. 134–5)

For Wittgenstein, our uses of language are dependent on our culture. This means that our view of language and our family resemblance concepts are cultural and cannot pretend to be universality. To understand concepts, we must understand the culture that created them. If we cannot understand the culture, we cannot understand its concepts (and vice versa). This notion of culture also involves a historical dimension, and Nietzsche often insists on the necessity of taking the historical or genealogical dimension into account. Values vary in space and time and language-games are dependent on these values. This is one way of understanding Wittgenstein's remark: 'If a lion could talk, we wouldn't be able to understand it' (PPF 327). The lion's concepts, values and whole culture, its 'form of life', would be so remote from ours that we would not be able to overcome the distance. The tribe Wittgenstein describes does not see that 'light blue' and 'dark blue' belong to the same family, shades of blue, but consider them as separate and distinct. They cannot see this family resemblance as they do not share our form of life.

Wittgenstein's focus on 'forms of life' brings to the fore the cultural dimension of language and goes against any essentialist understanding of it: language is a social and cultural practice which cannot be abstracted from this sociocultural ground. In his LA, Wittgenstein links once again language-game and culture: 'What belongs to a language game is a whole culture' (LA 26). The form of life to which a language belongs thus has an important sociocultural dimension, and Peter Hacker argues that this dimension can be found in Wittgenstein's use of the notion:

> §19 and §23 were concerned with emphasizing that language is a form of activity integrated in a way of living, §242 shifts focus. It is concerned with emphasizing the fact that the shared language of a community involves a deep and unquestioned agreement on the rules for the use of expressions of the language and on *what counts* as their correct use. It is obvious enough that in order for language to be used as a means of communication, there must be agreement on what the expressions of language mean. (Hacker 2015, 8)

The first dimension brings to the fore the active side of language – language is a practice, an ordinary activity – and the second the notion of agreement which grounds linguistic practice; language is a practice shared among people, and these people must agree on basic terms for the language to be functional. Indeed, if the players do not agree on the rules beforehand, they cannot play the game. If language is to be functional, speakers must agree not only on concepts and meanings but also on values. Some language-games aim at disturbing this ordinary agreement; poetry, for instance, functions precisely by modifying the uses of language (for instance by breaking sentences into lines in versified poems, or by playing with the sound of words and not only their place in the grammatical structure).

This focus on agreement and the blurred borders of concepts seem to lead to a form of conceptual relativism. If there are various forms of life and that any language-game is dependent on a form of life, then true and false are values only within one or another of these language-games. Once again, literature and poetry are places where true and false (understood in the context of a correspondence theory of truth) cannot apply. In other words, humans agree on a conceptual system or scheme which they follow. But this does not mean that the agreed conceptual scheme is the only and best possible one. Agreement is key for Wittgenstein: '"So you are saying that human agreement decides what is true and what is false?" – What is true or false is what human beings *say*; and it is in their *language* that human beings agree. This is agreement not in opinions, but rather in form of life' (PI 241). Truth and falsity only exist in language, in what humans say. Like Nietzsche, Wittgenstein nuances the notion of truth: to state that a proposition is true depends on the game which is played. To state that a proposition is true therefore reveals less of the proposition (for to attribute the value 'true' depends solely on the game) than of the game itself: it reveals one of the value judgements on which the game is built. A poetic statement such as 'la terre est bleue comme une orange' reveals less of the colour or the shape of the earth than of some idea of what poetry is.

A statement thus reveals the agreements the players have made: 'It is not only agreement in definitions, but also (odd as it may sound) agreement in judgements that is required for communication by means of language. This seems to abolish logic, but does not do so' (PI 242). Not only must the community of players agree on the use of words in order to communicate, but also agree on judgements. The agreements – and the form of life thereby established – do not only confer meanings to words but also values.

Obviously, if there are different language-games based on different forms of life, then logic might lose its primacy as a method of thinking. However, as Paul O'Grady argues, logic is not abolished but the uniqueness of the system of logic is abandoned: 'So rather than focussing on a single system of logic, Wittgenstein begins to explore the possibility that there may be quite different systems of logic' (O'Grady 2004, 318). Just as there might be different systems of logic, there are different language-games, and the most common ones reveal the most common values of a community or society. Nietzsche's revaluation of all values is, as we have seen, an attempt to change the nihilistic values on which culture is built; Nietzsche does not question truth itself, but the value we agree to give to it over untruth. On the contrary, Wittgenstein does not question this value but describes its relation to our agreements, our form of life, and therefore relativizes it: truth is not absolute but a value on which we agree.

The objection to Wittgenstein's pluralist view is that this variety opens the door to relativism – different forms of life might have different agreements on values – and Wittgenstein's problem with scepticism is certainly related to this issue. Wittgenstein can always escape this problem and rely on the agreement we share in our form of life. Truth might be dependent on our language, but inasmuch as this language is more or less fixed, as long as we agree on it, truth is not a relative notion. As O'Grady argues: 'There is a multiplicity possible in the conceptual systems by which we think about reality – but there isn't relativism about truth, incommensurability, or radical relativism about rationality' (O'Grady 2004, 335–6). Relativism concerns the conceptual system: different contexts or different cultures are based on various conceptual systems. Within one conceptual system – once it is agreed on, we could say – there is no space left for relativism. Moreover, and like Nietzsche's perspectivism, this does not mean that all conceptual systems are equal. Some are better suited than others to perform certain tasks. Truth, logic and reason are not absolute in the sense that they are relative to the conceptual system in which they are used. Within the conceptual system they can be granted an absolute dimension. Wittgenstein's moderate relativism would thus avoid some of the problems encountered by straightforward readings of Nietzsche's perspectivism. As we have seen in the previous chapter, Wittgenstein's pluralism and Nietzsche's perspectivism can be seen at establishing what Simon Blackburn calls a 'rolling pragmatism' in which we move from one practice to another.

In this context, Wittgenstein can thus be considered a conceptual relativist. His relativism does not concern how language works within practices, but the choice of the preferred language-game and form of life. As Maria Baghramian argues, what is common to all conceptual relativists 'is the rejection of realism on the one hand and cultural – or "anything goes" – versions of relativism, on the other' (Baghramian 2004, 187). The rejection of realism suggests that there is no world we can grasp outside of our conceptual scheme, and the rejection of cultural relativism suggests that there is a possibility of sharing world views. Wittgenstein escapes the problems of more radical versions of relativism (such as cultural relativism and relativism about rationality), and Nietzsche's perspectivism can be fruitfully read in a similar way to avoid problems of self-contradiction. We have seen that Nietzsche aims at revaluating the values we usually attribute to truth and reason for instance, and Wittgenstein's conception of language-games and their related forms of life can be interpreted as suggesting something similar. We have seen that, for Nietzsche, language serves to link a community together, and we can find the same emphasis on the sociocultural dimension in Wittgenstein's later works. Everyday communication is one practice among many others. Some practices reinforce values from everyday life whereas others try to bring us to change perspective. Art for instance – and poetry will be my focus in the next chapter because of its direct relation to language – aims precisely at disturbing our ordinary view and at bringing us to shift perspective.

Nietzsche's and Wittgenstein's views on language therefore share quite some characteristics with both *Romantic Expressivism*, from which they inherit, and *Pragmatic Expressivism*, which they influence (mainly Wittgenstein). However, they do not go as far as the Romantics in considering an absolute to lie in the literary or the poetic but do not either fall back into the rationalism of Brandom, Price and Blackburn. Their focus on the idea that language shapes the world and on the making of meaning brings to the fore the poetic component of expressivism, in the etymological sense of *poiesis*, and shows the closeness between the poetic and the pragmatic in the idea of making. This focus on the making of and in language is central to understanding the ways in which poetry can function, and this making of poetry will be the focus of the next two chapters. Nietzsche and Wittgenstein, or better the intersection between them, show a middle ground between *Romantic Expressivism* and

Pragmatic Expressivism in which the poetic is neither relegated to the suburbs of language nor considered the absolute centre, for there is no such centre. They unite Romanticism and pragmatism in a form of *Poetic Expressivism* that, as we will see, give tools to approach poetic phenomena from the perspective of philosophy of language.

5

Poetry after Nietzsche and Wittgenstein

A poetic philosophy of language can be found at the intersection of *Romantic Expressivism* and *Pragmatic Expressivism* – an intersection where Nietzsche and Wittgenstein connect to one another. In overcoming the opposition between philosophy and poetry, Nietzsche's and Wittgenstein's *Poetic Expressivism* shows a way to answer the challenges that poetry poses to philosophy of language and to bridge across the analytic–continental divide. Indeed, although this divide is, as we have seen, mainly a misrepresentation and a misunderstanding from both sides, it still retains an effectiveness in various fields of philosophical research, and especially in aesthetics. As mentioned, analytic and continental methodologies are so different in approaching aesthetic phenomena that it looks like they have radically different objects of study: a novel or a painting will not launch the same kind of reflection for an analytic or a continental philosopher. As Roger Pouivet describes it:

> Anglo-American aesthetics thus appears as a branch of other subjects and, especially, of analytic metaphysics. This has sometimes led 'continental' philosophers to think that it does not focus enough on the works themselves, that it has wandered from their real history, from the sociological conditions of their appearance, from the critical judgments one can pass on them. [. . .] To me this criticism seems to rely on a contradiction concerning the general project of Anglo-American aesthetics. This project does not aim so much at reaching a global interpretation of the phenomenon of art – which is sometimes called 'metaphysics of art' – but rather at evaluating the various argumentations at play on delineated issues. (Pouivet 2000, 47)

According to Pouivet, analytic aesthetics thus approaches and solves specific problems related to art whereas continental aesthetics is a more generalized attempt at understanding the role and significance of art. In other words, it is the scope of inquiry that differs: analytic aesthetics is concerned with 'delineated' problems whereas continental aesthetics takes a more global approach.

Looking more specifically at the philosophy of literature, the divide has something to do with the relation to language, and hence to the conception of language one holds. As Peter Kivy argues, the turn to language in philosophy has not been helpful to aesthetics, quite to the contrary:

> Nor was the newly emerging school of linguistic analysis, in its various forms, the savior of aesthetics. To the contrary, if anything, it passed an even harsher judgment on the discipline than did the positivists. For whereas the positivists were more or less content to give it a dismissive shrug in the direction of the 'emotive,' the language analysts took special pains to exclude aesthetics, not with a whimper but with a bang. (Kivy 2004, 2)

Most analytic philosophers of literature have inherited from the 'linguistic turn' and therefore consider literature from the point of view of a representational conception of language, focusing on aspects such as the relation between truth and fiction or the specificities of literary language. On the contrary, continental aesthetics does not focus on such linguistic problems and understands literature as something more general, as describing a way of relating to the world. Stanley Cavell is one of the rare philosophers to approach specific problems in philosophy of literature while keeping a broader spectrum in mind. In this context, he takes into account the double direction of the genitive in the locution philosophy *of* literature and questions not only the impacts of philosophy on literature but also those of literature on philosophy, as he asks in the closing question to his *Claim of Reason*: 'Can philosophy become literature and still know itself?' (Cavell 1979, 496). In this sense, Cavell makes a move towards understanding the poetics of philosophy in the way literature affects philosophical discourse.

By focusing specifically on poetry, I aim to show in this chapter that the *Poetic Expressivism* built on Nietzsche and Wittgenstein offers a way of approaching poetry from the perspective of philosophy of language. Against the idea that philosophy of language and poetry are obstacles to one another, I argue that a philosophy of poetry offers a poetic philosophy of language (rather than a philosophy of poetic language). In this chapter, I therefore aim to move away from an essentialist definition of poetry to a wider family resemblance concept of poetics (which could therefore be applied to art forms other than poetry), and this occurs in the specific use of language that one finds in poetry. In this sense, I am moving from a representational poetics to an expressive one, as Jacques Rancière argues:

> There are only two kinds of poetics: a representative poetics that determines the genre and generic perfection of poems on the basis of their invention of a fable; and an expressive poetics that determines them as direct expressions of the poetic power. A normative poetics says how poems should be made; a historical poetics says how they are made, that is, in the end, how they express the state of things, language, and manners that gave them birth. (Rancière 2011, 67)

While a representational poetics searches for the ontology of poetry and aims to determine whether this or that poem belongs to the category 'poetry', an expressive poetics focuses on the relation between the poem and the world, on what the poem reveals of the world. In other words, inasmuch as representational language helps us name things in the world by linking objects and categories, representational poetics tells us how to classify a poem among various genres. On the contrary, an expressive poetics is not focused on meaning *qua* reference but on understanding the significance of poetry.

This chapter is divided into three parts: first, I consider Nietzsche's poetry and relate his Apollonian/Dionysian distinction to the opposition between representation and expression explored in the previous chapters; second, I turn to Wittgenstein's remarks on understanding poetry, thus shifting from the making of poetry to its reception; third, I explore what is at play in reading poetry, showing that poetry can be considered a form of reading-as following Wittgenstein's seeing-as.

1 Nietzsche's poetry and the inversion of Platonism

By rejecting metaphysics *qua* Platonism, Nietzsche is not only rejecting representationalism but also Plato's banishing of poetry. In an early note, he considers his philosophy to be an inverted Platonism: 'My philosophy is an inverted Platonism: the further something is from true being, the purer, the more beautiful, the better it is. Living in illusion as the goal' (KSA7:7[156]). This inversion therefore brings Nietzsche to adopt an attitude towards poetry fundamentally opposed to Plato's: rather than criticizing the poet's distance from truth, Nietzsche praises it because the whole idea of the 'Truth' is misleading according to him. By reinstating poetry in the philosophical realm, Nietzsche also embraces the poetics of philosophy: his philosophical writings have an undoubtedly poetic dimension and he also writes poems himself.

His poem 'Only fool, only poet!' responds to Plato's banishing of poetry from the realm of truth:

> 'Der *Wahrheit* Freier – du?' so höhnten sie / 'nein! nur ein Dichter!' / ein Thier, ein listiges, raubendes, schleichendes, / das lügen muss, / das wissentlich, willentlich lügen muss, / nach Beute lüstern, / bunt verlarvt, / sich selbst zur Larve, / sich selbst zur Beute / *das* – der Wahrheit Freier? . . . / Nur Narr! Nur Dichter! / Nur Buntes redend, / aus Narrenlarven bunt herausredend, / herumsteigend auf lügnerischen Wortbrücken, / auf Lügen-Regenbogen / zwischen falschen Himmeln / herumschweifend, herumschleichend – / *nur* Narr! *nur* Dichter! . . .

> 'The free truth – you?' They scoffed / 'No! Only a poet!' / A nasty, robbing, and crawling animal, / Who must lie, / Must wisely, willingly lie, / Lusting for booty, / Colorfully disguised, / Who is the masque, / Who is the booty himself, / Is *that* – the free truth? . . . / Only fool! Only poet! / Only colorful speaking, / From a colourful larval fool, / Climbing upon false broken / Words and false rainbows / Between false heavens / Crawling and creeping – / *Only* fool! *Only* poet! (DD, 'Only Fool!' / KSA 6.377-378)

Nietzsche's poem stages the poet as a fool, therefore restating Plato's conception of the poet as irrational. The poet is a fool to think that she has something to do with truth. The translation of 'der Wahrheit Freier' as 'the free truth' is problematic but interesting. It is problematic because 'Freier' does not mean free and is not an adjective. This translation therefore inverts the syntactical relation between 'Wahrheit' and 'Freier'. Richard Hollingdale translates it as 'the wooer of truth' and Walter Kaufmann as 'the suiter of truth' which both maintain the correct grammatical relation between 'Wahrheit' and 'Freier' and present the poet as aiming towards the same goal as the philosopher, that is, searching for truth. Although linguistically incorrect, the notion of freedom is, however, interesting as it could suggest that the poet is free from this idea of truth whereas the philosopher is still bound to it, in the opposition between the poet's expressivism and the philosopher's representationalism. Following these notions of love and freedom, the poet would therefore be the one who loves truth and who also frees others from it. The others, however, only reply

'Only fool! Only Poet!' and do not take her seriously. Two criticisms are made to poets here: first, they are liars, and this follows Plato's idea that the poets move away from truth, and, second, their words are only colourful speaking, not serious speaking, thus anticipating Frege's dismissal of the 'colouring' in determining meaning and Austin's rejection of poetry in the realm of the non-serious.

By distancing herself from truth as correspondence, by knowingly lying, the poet might get closer to another kind of truth as Nietzsche suggests in a note that elaborates on the chapter 'Poets' from TSZ:

> Der Dichter, der lügen kann / wissentlich, willentlich, / der kann allein Wahrheit reden.
>
> The poet, who can / willingly and knowingly lie, / can alone tell the truth. (KSA 11:28[20])

The poet's conscious lie becomes a way of telling the truth. Although this claim seems contradictory at first glance, it in fact opposes two kinds of truth: truth as correspondence and truth as disclosure. By lying in the sense of truth as correspondence, the poet is disclosing something of the world. We have seen that this concept of disclosure is also problematic in the sense that it suggests that something hidden needs to be disclosed, but we can understand it as a way of making sense of the world, of giving significance to the world rather than uncovering a hidden truth, therefore moving away from metaphysics (reaching what lies behind the world of appearances) to pragmatics (living in the world of appearances).

Further in 'Only Fool, Only Poet', Nietzsche pursues this distinction through the oppositions between truth and untruth, rationality and irrationality, in terms of day and night or light and darkness:

> Bei abgehellter Luft, / wenn schon des Monds Sichel/ grün zwischen Pupurröthen/ und neidisch hinschleicht, / – dem Tage feind, / mit jedem Schritte heimlich / an Rosen-Hängematten / hinsichelnd, bis sie sinken, / nachtabwärts blass hinabsinken: / so sank ich selber einstmals, / aus meinem Wahrheits-Wahnsinne, / aus meinen Tages-Sehnsüchten, / des Tages müde, / krank vom Lichte, / – sank abwärts, abendwärts, schattenwärts, / von Einer Wahrheit / verbrannt und durstig / – gedenkst du noch, gedenkst du, heisses Herz, / wie da du durstetest? – / dass ich verbannt sei / von aller Wahrheit! / *Nur* Narr! *Nur* Dichter! . . .

> Near an opaque sky, / The crescent moon / Crawls across crimson / And creeps enviously / – the enemy of Day, / With each secret step toward / The hanging rose gardens / Hobbling, until it sinks / With the death of the night: / So I myself once sank / From my truth and delusion, / From my Day-searching / Tired of day, sick of light, / I sank down, deepen into the shadows, / Burned and thirsty / from every truth / – Do you still remember, remember, hot heart, / How you once thirsted there? / I was banished/ from all Truth! / Only fool! Only poet! (DD, 'Only Fool!' / KSA 6.380)

Nietzsche's poet remembers the Platonic days when she was banished from the realm of truth. This image represents the poet as going down or sinking in Plato's cave, far away from the sun which represents the truth in Plato's allegory but also, interestingly, stages the poet as making this move willingly, although the term 'sinking' is ambiguous in that regard. This idea parallels Zarathustra's journey: at the beginning of the book he decides to go down from his mountain into the 'human' world and thus begins Zarathustra's 'Untergang', usually translated as 'going under' but which also means sinking or decline.[1]

Nietzsche's staging of the poet moving away from truth is a move away from truth as correspondence. Moving away from the metaphysical and representational framework of Plato's philosophy, Nietzsche turns his attention to the poet. In so doing, Nietzsche is moving away from representationalism and towards expressivism. This tension between representation and expression can be conceptualized through his opposition between Apollo and Dionysus in BT: Apollo is the god of appearance and image, whereas Dionysus is the god of expression and music. In TI Nietzsche considers the two types of intoxication that Apollo and Dionysus represent:

> Apollonian intoxication keeps the eye in particular aroused, so that it receives visionary power. The painter, the sculptor, the epic poet are visionaries *par excellence*. In the Dionysian state, on the other hand, the whole system of the emotions is aroused and intensified: so that it discharges its very means of expression at one stroke, at the same time forcing out the power to represent, reproduce, transfigure, transform, every kind of mime and play-acting. (TI 'Skirmishes' 10 / KSA 6.117)

Apollonian art forms therefore rely on the power of vision whereas Dionysian ones force out the idea of imitation by privileging expression. Tragedy for Nietzsche must combine and balance between Apollonian and Dionysian, between representation and expression. For Nietzsche tragedy must not be limited to drama, and we will see that poetry is very close to tragedy in Nietzsche's understanding of it. In a similar way, we will see that Wittgenstein's distinction and combination of two kinds of understanding (one that can be paraphrased and the other that cannot) in PI 531 opposes once again designation and expression, representation and music. Wittgenstein's attempt at combining these two kinds of understanding work towards achieving the same task: to elaborate a conception of language which can balance between the two poles, which can encompass the various language-games as a family of practices. As we have seen, Nietzsche's and Wittgenstein's aim is neither to embrace *Romantic Expressivism* nor to fall into the rationalism of *Pragmatic Expressivism*, but to find a middle ground between the two.

Nietzsche's conception of poetry is therefore inscribed in the broader view of his anti-Platonism and of his understanding of Greek tragedy in BT. The distinction between representation and expression was indeed already at play in the Greek's conceptions of language, according to Nietzsche:

> Here we find sketched out for us the only possible relationship between poetry and music, between word and sound: the word, the image, the concept, seeks an expression analogous to music and now feels the force of music in itself. In this sense we may distinguish two main currents in the history of language of the Greek people, according to whether language imitates the world of phenomena and images or the world of music. (BT 6 / KSA 1.49)

Nietzsche separates the history of language in ancient Greece into two trends: one towards image and one towards music. Nietzsche thus distinguishes between a theory of language based on image – language is the representation of the world, the picture theory of meaning – and one based on music – language is the expression of the world. As we have seen, Nietzsche criticizes the representational conception of language as being too metaphysical. However, like Wittgenstein, Nietzsche does not attempt to reject language as representation completely but to focus on the fact that it is not the only way one can consider language and that we must reject the primacy we usually give to language as representation. Nietzsche takes tragedy as the best example of this dual conception of language because it combines both representation and expression. Nietzsche considers poetry as having this duality as well, combining images and music in the text. To analyse tragedy and its constitutive duality, Nietzsche takes Apollo as the god of representation and Dionysus as the god of expression. Tragedy comes from the union of Apollo and Dionysus, and these contrary forces must remain in an equilibrium for tragedy to exist.

Tragedy is closely related to poetry for Nietzsche insofar as in poetry, too, the words must both represent and express. Nietzsche considers Schiller to be a good example for a 'musical poet': 'For [Schiller] admitted that in the preparatory state which precedes the act of writing poetry he did not have before him and within him a series of images and casually organized thoughts, but rather a *musical mood*' (BT 5 / KSA 1.43). But a poem is not merely a musical mood; it is a succession of words which all have some kind of relation to images. In that sense, poetry is neither a purely expressive art form nor a purely representational one (and one might argue that no art form is pure in that regard).

One important question remains, however: if poetry has an expressive dimension, what is its relation to truth? We have seen that there can be no truth as correspondence when one abandons language as representation, and, in TL, Nietzsche's critique of truth is a critique of the correspondence theory of truth and the value we give it (i.e. believing it is the only truth, whereas Nietzsche aims to show that truth is also a sociocultural and moral construct). What truth is left once correspondence is gone? According to Nietzsche, poetry is closer to truth because it avoids the traps of metaphysical language:

> The sphere of poetry does not lie outside the world, as the fantastic impossibility imagined by the brain of a poet: it wants to be the very opposite, the unadorned expression of truth, and must therefore cast off the deceitful finery of the supposed reality of the man of culture. (BT8 / KSA 1.58)

Whereas poetry is often considered as being outside the world, as being an imaginative creation that sprang out of the poet's mind, as something maybe pleasant but never true, Nietzsche turns the relation between poetry and truth upside down and considers poetry as the expression of truth. Nietzsche's reversal of the relation between poetry and truth leads him to consider poetry as being 'the unadorned expression of truth' and representational language as deceitful. Nietzsche's use of the term 'unadorned' suggests that, for Nietzsche, against the commonplace idea that poetic language is ornamental, the language of poetry in fact responds to a necessity of expression that makes sense of the world rather than hiding behind the 'deceitful finery' of culture. But if the poet is the one who makes sense of the world, what is the role played by the readers?

2 Wittgenstein on understanding poetry

Shifting our focus from the poet to the reader also shifts our attention from Nietzsche to Wittgenstein. For Wittgenstein too, the musical and expressive dimensions of poetic language play an important role: 'The way music speaks. Do not forget that a poem, even though it is composed in the language of information, is not used in the language-game of giving information' (Z 160). There is a similarity between understanding music and understanding poetry, for they both are a particular language. Understanding a poem cannot occur on the same grounds as understanding information; as we will see, information can be paraphrased, whereas poetry cannot. This does not mean that there is some content or a message in informative uses of language and none in poetic uses, nor that in poetic uses the form is the message, but that this notion of message relies on representationalism. Poetry is the place par excellence in which form and content fuse: there is no such thing as a message in poetry if by message we understand something separated from its vehicle of transmission. What poetry shows is that message and vehicle, content and form, are one, and that such an identity is also at work in ordinary language, although to a lesser extent.[2] Wittgenstein's discussion of private language and the notion of pain can be seen as pointing towards this idea that meaning cannot be construed as an information package that can be transmitted from one person to another in expressive language-games.

Even though language sometimes works on the grounds of representation (or rather can be seen from the perspective of representation), it is not always the case. What distinguishes poetry from representational language is neither the content nor the words, but only the use of these words. To understand Wittgenstein's remark from Z, it is important to grasp the distinction between language and language-game. What is a language of information? And what is a language-game of information? Wittgenstein suggests a shift from semantics to pragmatics: the distinction between poetic and ordinary language does not happen at the level of language but at that of the language-game. The distinction between poetic and ordinary is not a metaphysical distinction between two kinds of language but a pragmatic one between uses of language. The distinction does not operate on the words used but on the ways the words are used. In this sense, poetic language is not purely expressive just as ordinary language is not purely representational: both representation and expression are at work in language, but poetry is one of the fields in which their combination is the most visible. As Henri Meschonnic argues:

> Both poetry and ordinary language come to being in the non-separation between sound and sense, as opposed to the sign model that misses a great part of linguistic empiricism. In all language activities, in a trivial way, speech comes first and not the unit word – which is where the separation between sound and sense takes place. A poem only begins when a serial semantics is at work in a speech, in a non-separation between affect and concept. (Meschonnic 2001, 31)[3]

The non-separation from affect and concept brings back the combination of representation and expression in language. A purely representational language can only be achieved in the dictionary, when one focuses on the word rather than speech. The language of information is not ordinary language: it constitutes the pool of words we ordinarily know and use. The language-game of information, to the contrary, is the ordinary language, the one we use in our everyday activities.[4]

Pursuing the relation between poetry and music, Wittgenstein considers the notion of understanding in PI 527 and following. More specifically, he compares understanding a sentence to understanding a musical theme and opposes musical themes to sentences. PI 531 to 533 focus on important elements to conceptualize poetic language:

> We speak of understanding a sentence in the sense in which it can be replaced by another which says the same; but also in the sense in which it cannot be replaced by any other. (Any more than one musical theme can be replaced by another.)
>
> In the one case, the thought in the sentence is what is common to different sentences; in the other, something that is expressed only by these words in these positions. (Understanding a poem.) (PI 531)

This remark brings forward an important problem in approaching poetry and poetic meaning: the problem of paraphrase. In *Must We Mean What We Say?* Stanley Cavell uses Wittgenstein to tackle the problem of paraphrase inherited from Cleanth Brooks's view in 'The Heresy of Paraphrase' according to which a poem cannot be paraphrased. Cavell takes the example of metaphors which can be paraphrased because they can be understood and explained. In explaining a metaphor (or to a wider extent a poem), I give a paraphrase. 'In summary: Brooks is wrong to say that poems cannot in principle be fully paraphrased, but right to be worried about the relation between paraphrase and poem' (Cavell 1976, 82). The relation between paraphrase and poem brings up the fact that understanding and explaining poetry is somehow different from understanding and explaining in ordinary language because there is a double understanding going on in metaphors and poems: 'I must understand the ordinary or dictionary meaning of the words it contains, *and* understand that they are not there being used in their ordinary way, that the meanings they invite are not to be found opposite them in a dictionary' (Cavell 1976, 79). Wittgenstein already affirms the impossibility of paraphrasing a poem in PG: 'No one would believe that a poem remained *essentially unaltered* if its words were replaced by others in accordance with an appropriate convention' (PG 32). This question of paraphrase is important because it conditions the possibility of translation: '(Who says that this English poem can be translated into German to our satisfaction?!) (Even *if* it is clear that there is in *some* sense a translation of any English sentence into German.)' (RFM 85) There is a way in which the poem can be translated, but the translation can never be the same as the original. Translation and paraphrase are similar in the sense that they give an idea of what the poem is about, of what its significance is, but can never replace the experiencing of the poem itself (or at least the experience of reading a translation is always different from the experience of reading the original version).

Wittgenstein therefore sees two possibilities in understanding a sentence: either a sentence can be explained by another (enabling the possibility of paraphrase), as it seems to be the case in the language-game of information; or it cannot, as it seems to be the case in music. Indeed, a musical phrase cannot be explained by a different musical phrase. The phrase itself is the only possible one; the only explanation is repetition. This type of sentence is not limited to musical phrases as Wittgenstein notes in parenthesis that understanding a poem follows the same lines. We must, however, nuance the idea that the only possible paraphrase for a poem is its repetition as, following Cavell, interpretation (or criticism as he puts it) is a way of paraphrasing a poem, an attempt in expressing the significance of the poem with different words. Poetry, unlike music, is written in the language of information but understanding a poem does not follow the same rules as understanding a proposition. As for music, an important aspect of poetry is the place given to words; not only the place in a sentence but also the place on the page (as for instance in Mallarmé's *Un coup de dés*). As musical phrases present these notes at these times, poetic sentences present 'these words in these positions'.

In PI 532, Wittgenstein considers 'understanding' to have the two different meanings we noted, paraphrasing and repeating: 'Then has "understanding" two different meanings here? – I would rather say that these kinds of use of "understanding" make up its meaning, make up my *concept* of understanding. For I *want* to apply the word "understanding" to all this' (PI 532). There are two kinds of understanding which build up the concept of understanding. In a similar way to Nietzsche's attempt at combining Apollo and Dionysus rather than separating them, Wittgenstein does not distinguish the concept of understanding in the everyday use from the concept of understanding in the poetic use. He does not split language into two different domains: the ordinary and the poetic. There is only one concept of understanding, and it must be able to consider both information and poetry, according to the perspective taken on language. Language is not constituted by different entities (such as ordinary, poetic and scientific), but by various perspectives which focus on one or another feature. Each language-game highlights one or another aspect of language, and Wittgenstein gives a clue as to how understanding is at work in poetic language-games in PI 533:

> But in the second case, how can one explain the expression, communicate what one understands? Ask yourself: How does one *lead* someone to understand a poem or a theme? The answer to this tells us how one explains the sense here. (PI 533)

Wittgenstein's answer is another question. We already know that one type of understanding, paraphrasing, cannot provide an explanation of a poem. And if Wittgenstein does not give a clear answer regarding how to understand a poem, he does point out something important in his question. To help someone understand a poem means to explain its meaning. But how does one explain the meaning of a poem? One shows how to look at it. Understanding a poem is a matter of perspective; one must look at it the right way. But if poetry is a language-game asking for a change of perspectives, what are the rules for this game?

3 Reading poetry

One needs to look at a poem in the right way in order to understand it, and this notion of 'looking' brings up another of Wittgenstein's concepts: 'seeing-as'. As Wittgenstein notices, 'seeing-as' often occurs in aesthetic reflections (RPP 1, PPF 178). This is especially the case concerning visual art forms, probably because of the word 'seeing'. However, Wittgenstein clearly distinguishes 'seeing-as' from 'seeing' (PPF 137), the former being 'half visual experience half thought' (PPF 140). Being 'half thought', art forms which are not primarily visual can also be grasped under this notion, and Wittgenstein's remarks on music and 'hearing-as' or 'playing-as' go in this direction. This notion can also be used to conceptualize what is at play in poetry, where 'seeing-as' becomes 'reading-as'.

In his *Lecture on Aesthetics*, Wittgenstein takes up this question of how poetry should be read:

> Take the question: 'How should poetry be read? What is the correct way of reading it?' If you are talking about blank verse the right way might of reading it might be stressing it correctly – you discuss how far you should stress the rhythm and how far you should hide it. A man says it ought to be read *this* way and reads it to you. You say: 'Oh yes. Now it makes sense.' [...] I had an experience with the 18th century poet Klopstock. I found that the way to read him was to stress his metre abnormally. Klopstock put ∪–∪ (etc.) in front of his poems. When I read his poems in this new way, I said: 'Ah-ha, now I know why he did this.' (LA 12)

There are ways of reading poetry which make more sense, and the poet, like Klopstock, might give a few hints on how the poem should be read. Other poets, to the contrary, give no instructions at all, leaving the reader free to read as she likes. But this entails that there are different ways of reading: there are different interpretations. This notion of interpretation, which is central in art criticism, is, Wittgenstein suggests, related to 'seeing-as': 'But we can also *see* the illustration now as one thing, now as another. – So we interpret it, and *see* it as we *interpret* it' (PPF 116). There is interpretation in 'seeing-as', just as there is interpretation in 'reading-as'. But how can we know how to read? Poetry requires from the reader that she stresses the words in a way different from everyday reading. A poem makes sense only once it is read in the right way. We should not understand 'right way' as something too specific: there can be multiple right ways to read a poem, more precisely, the right way to read a poem is the one that makes sense for the reader. It might make sense to read in this way but not in that way. This idea could be called 'reading-as', following Wittgenstein's 'seeing-as': a duck-rabbit can be seen as a duck or as a rabbit; a poem can be read as a meaningless series of words or as a meaningful whole.[5] Another interesting aspect of this quote is the reference to Klopstock. Although the reader is free to read the poem as she likes, the poet can indicate how it should be read and Klopstock does so by indicating the rhythm. Reading a poem in one way might not make sense whereas reading it following the instructions does. In that sense, a poem is subject to interpretation. Its meaning varies according to how the readers read it. More than that, it shows a different use of language. Reading a poem and reading a newspaper both involve reading, but not in the same sense. This difference is similar to Wittgenstein's distinction between seeing and 'seeing-as'.

The poetic language-game, or better the poetic language-games for there is more than one way of doing poetry, brings light on different aspects of language, aspects which are not highlighted in the ordinary communicational practice. In a way, poetry resembles Duchamp's ready-mades: Duchamp takes an everyday object and transforms its meaning by placing it in a different game, in a different context. Similarly, poets take everyday words and transform their meaning. There is a poetic transformation (or transfiguration in Arthur Danto's sense) of the everyday. For instance, in his poem 'Two Pendants: For the Ears', William Carlos Williams inserts a grocery list (Williams 2000, 166). What is more ordinary than a grocery list? The fact that it is written by a poet and presented as a poem brings us, readers, to believe there is something more to it, to read it as a poem. I believe it could work as an autonomous text, but Williams's poem is part of a larger poem. Taken in the wider context of the whole poem, the grocery list appears as a bursting in of the ordinary in the poetic, and its place within a poem makes of this all too ordinary grocery list something poetic.

The ordinary brings a poetic element despite its ordinary dimension. What is interesting in the apparition of the ordinary within the poetic is not only that the ordinary becomes poetic but also and above all that the poem stages this ordinary becoming poetic and, by doing so, abolishes any essential difference between ordinary and poetic. The most ordinary words, the most ordinary sentences can become poetic in a certain context.[6] The context of the poem transforms the ordinary grocery list into a poetic element. In his poem *Paterson*, Williams comments on his use of a grocery list and considers that treating such a list rhythmically makes it poetic (Williams 2013, 261). It is therefore a certain attention to rhythm that transforms an ordinary text into a poem, in the same way that for Wittgenstein the poetic dimension arises from reading with a certain rhythm. Williams further considers that the difficulty in poetry lies in the fact that the meaning of words is not limited to 'the common sense of what it says' (Williams 2013, 262). In poetry, rhythm and sound add something to the ordinary meaning of words.

Rhythm is one aspect which can change the perspective on words, another possible one is sound. In the poem 'The Crate' (Ponge 1974, 34), Francis Ponge plays on the similarity between the sounds of the word 'crate': the French *cageot* (crate) sounds similar to *cage* (cage) and *cachot* (cell). Ponge describes this very ordinary object by playing on the sound of the word, thus relating the meaning of the crate to those of the cage and the cell. By connecting these meanings, he can attribute adjectives used to describe human beings in cells to fruits in a crate. For instance, the terms 'fall sick' and 'suffocation' are related to the idea of the cell and transposed onto the crate. The sound of ordinary words thus becomes the playground for the emergence of the poetic in what looks like a very ordinary descriptive sentence. These examples show ways in which poetry can modify the ordinary or, better, how poetry can arise or appear within the most ordinary words. An important dimension in this change of meaning is the context in which the word or the object appears. Depending on the context, the meaning changes. By displacing a sentence or a statement from an ordinary context to a poetic one, the poet, to some extent, makes the ordinary extraordinary.[7]

The grocery list example is the inscription of an ordinary text within a poetic one. Another poem by Williams, 'This Is Just to Say' (Williams 2000, 72–3), operates a similar move, but it is no longer the inscription of the ordinary within the poetic which grants a poetic status to the ordinary text, but the inscription of an ordinary text, or rather a seemingly ordinary one, as a whole in a collection of poems. 'This Is Just to Say' could very well be a note hung on the fridge (here is another similarity with the grocery list), but by moving it from the fridge to the collection of poems, Williams changes its status. These examples of poems all go in the same direction, namely that there is no essential difference between ordinary and poetic language, and that the specificity of poetry is not to be found in specific words or sentence constructions, but that the poetic always lies at the heart of ordinary language, as Stanley Fish argues: 'What philosophical semantics and the philosophy of speech acts are telling us is that ordinary language is extraordinary because at its heart is precisely the realm of values, intentions, and purposes which is often assumed to be the exclusive property of literature' (Fish 1982, 108). Fish's idea is interesting because it breaks down the difference between ordinary and poetic language and does not attempt to define literature as a use of language whose essential characteristics are fundamentally different from ordinary speech. What is at play in literature for Fish, and that goes in the direction of what Wittgenstein says, is that literature is a matter of context or perspective.

One can see something in different ways, giving various interpretations, and these interpretations all depend on the context in which she sees this thing, or the context she creates around it:

> I can imagine some arbitrary cipher – this, ℋ for instance, to be a strictly correct letter of some foreign alphabet. Or again, to be a faultily written one, and faulty in this way or that: for example, it might be slapdash, or typical childish awkwardness, or, like the flourishes in an official document. It could deviate from the correctly written letter in a variety of ways. – And according to the fiction with which I surround it, I can see it in various aspects. And here there is a close kinship with 'experiencing the meaning of a word.' (PPF 234)

Interestingly, the word 'fiction' translates to the German *Erdichtung* which contains the root *Dichtung*, poetry. The fiction (or the poetic invention) names the context. When there is no given context, when an object stands out and cannot be attached back to its original background, one must therefore create a context in which the object makes or takes sense. Of course, an object is never seen out of any context, and one can usually easily attach an object to the everyday world. But it can also happen that one finds an object and does not recognize it. She will therefore build fictions in order to find the use for the object. This also applies to works of art: a painting, whether seen in a museum or in a church, can be subject to various interpretations. The same applies to a poem, whether read in its original context or in a different one (in the original anthology or in a textbook for instance). As Fish argues: 'communication occurs within situations and [. . .] to be in a situation is already to be in possession of (or to be possessed by) a structure of assumptions, of practices understood to be relevant in relation to purposes and goals that are already in place; and it is within the assumption of these purposes and goals that any utterance is *immediately* heard' (Fish 1982, 318). Understanding a poem, or any kind of linguistic understanding, is situated. The situation, or the context, provides a set of assumptions that are tested. When there is a problem, the reader must be creative and 'surround' the word, the sentence, the sign, by a fiction in order to make sense.

For Wittgenstein, this importance of fiction and context links 'seeing-as' to 'experiencing the meaning of a word'. Noticing an aspect is identifying an element in a larger picture, among various other elements, just as 'experiencing the meaning of a word' is identifying its use among the many possible ones. One art form in which experiencing meanings is central is poetry, and Wittgenstein brings up this comparison:

> 'When I read a poem or narrative with feeling, surely something goes on in me which does not go on when I merely skim the lines for information.' – What processes am I alluding to? – The sentences have a different *ring*. I pay careful attention to intonation. Sometimes a word has the wrong intonation, stands out too much or too little. [. . .] I can also give a word an intonation which makes its meaning stand out from the rest, almost as if the word were a portrait of the whole thing. (And this may, of course, depend on the structure of the sentence.) (PPF 264)

Poetry, or any other 'creative' use of language, draws attention to something which does not occur in the everyday language-game. In poetry, intonation makes a word stand out from the rest; this word gains an 'outstanding' meaning which differs from its meaning in the everyday use and an 'outstanding' position which differs from that of the other words. As we have seen, Wittgenstein relates the understanding of a poem to the positions of the words in PI 531. What matters in poetry is the position of the words, and one cannot change them without changing the meaning of the poem. Understanding a poem differs from understanding a sentence in the everyday language-game as we have seen: in the everyday one, it is possible to paraphrase; in poetry, the only paraphrase is repetition or, following Cavell, interpretation and criticism.

Poetry is a specific language-game in which understanding does not follow the rules of the everyday one. It is a game with language which must be understood in its context. Poetic and ordinary languages must, however, not be considered as two distinct entities. The poetic is a language-game, a practice which must be recognized as such. According to Peter Lamarque, the practice of poetry is governed by rules on which poets and readers agree: 'Poetry is constituted by a practice, which is grounded in convention-governed expectations among poets and readers' (Gibson 2015, 33). One limit to such a conception of poetry, and one of the reasons why poetry seems to always defy definition is that poetry, especially in the twentieth century, challenges the established conventions and expectations. In this sense, the practice of poetry would rely on the convention that it disturbs and challenges established conventions. The reader who approaches a poem cannot always rely on the tools she usually uses to understand poetry but might be brought to find new ways of approaching it, new tools to engage in an interpretative process. In other words, and as Fish argues, the interpreter who engages in such a practice makes the poem: 'Interpretation is not the art of construing but the art of constructing. Interpreters do not decode poems; they make them' (Fish 1982, 327). Just as I sometimes need to create a fiction around something for it to make sense, in interpreting a poem I have to create the conditions or situation for this interpretation to make sense. Interpretation is thus central in 'seeing-as', but it calls for another more creative notion: imagination: 'In other words, the concept "Now I see it as . . ." is related to "Now I am imagining *that*"' (PPF 254).

Through the importance of imagination, poetry is a game that can be likened to the children's game Wittgenstein describes in PPF 205-207 in which the children take a chest for a house. We have seen that interpretation depends on a context which can be understood as the fiction created around an object. The same happens with children playing: they weave 'a piece of fancy around [the chest]', they create a context in which the meaning is not the same, in which the interpretation of the object does not follow the lines of the everyday language-game. 'Seeing-as' is to some extent similar to interpreting. But the children's game example shows another aspect of 'seeing-as': it is also similar to imagining. To take the chest for a house does not call for interpretation but for imagination. Wittgenstein's discussion of imagination brings the creative dimension of 'seeing-as' to the fore and its relation to the will: 'Seeing an aspect and imagining are subject to the will' (PPF 256). Imagination enables us not only to describe a change of aspect (as with interpretation) but to create it. This dimension reinforces the link between 'seeing-as' and the work of an artist. If a poet interprets the world to create her poem, she also needs imagination to do so. As Charles Altieri suggests, in matters of Wittgensteinian literary aesthetics, imagination is an essential feature (Altieri 2015, 59–62).

Just like the children's game, poetry is a game in which the meanings of the words are changed. Insofar as the chest becomes a house for the children, the meanings the poet uses for a word become this word's meaning. This creation of new meanings is also used in everyday language, but poetry represents a stage on which this creation is brought to a greater degree. More than creating new meanings, poetry highlights possible uses of language, thus giving them a significance that we overlook in our everyday speech, as Wittgenstein suggests: 'We don't notice the enormous variety of all the everyday language-games, because the clothing of our language makes them all alike' (PPF 335). There are many language-games, but we do not notice them all. One of the characteristics of poetic language-games is that they reveal themselves as language-games, as games on or with language. This game is based on noticing aspects which can take different meanings according to which game is being played. But the external appearance does not change; all language-games use the same material: words. And the meanings of these words vary according to their use, the language-game in which they appear. A poetic use of language might use a word in a yet unknown way, and by doing so poetry reveals aspects of words and of the world we did not know, just as 'a good simile refreshes the intellect' (CV, p. 3). A poetic use of language will therefore not necessarily bring a new meaning to a word or sentence but bring this word or sentence to gain a new significance, to make sense of the world in a different way.

6

Towards a perspectival poetics

That poetry requires a kind of reading-as modelled on Wittgenstein's seeing-as reveals that the difference between ordinary and poetic language is not one of kind (ontological, semantic or syntactic) but one of perspective and interpretation (pragmatic). Poetry, and other art forms, by forcing us to 'noticing aspects', asks that we look with a perspective that will highlight features of the world we might have otherwise overlooked.[1] A note from Wittgenstein's CV brings up this notion of perspective in art:

> Let's imagine a theatre, the curtain goes up & we see someone alone in his room walking up and down, lighting a cigarette, seating <u>himself</u> etc. so that suddenly we are observing a human being from outside in a way that ordinarily we can never observe ourselves; as if we were watching a chapter from a biography with our own eyes, – surely this would be at once uncanny and wonderful. More wonderful than anything that a playwright could cause to be acted or spoken on the stage. – But then we do see this every day & it makes not the slightest impression on us! True enough, but we do not see it from *that* point of view. [. . .] The work of art compels us – as one might say – to see it in the <u>right</u> perspective, but without art the object is a piece of nature like any other & the fact that *we* may exalt it through our enthusiasm does not give anyone the right to display it to us. (CV, p. 7, underline in original)

Just as everyday language does not make much impression on us, precisely because we use it every day, a scene from everyday life does not surprise us. Once transposed on stage, however, this scene takes another dimension, just like the poet gives to words a dimension they did not previously have. It is in this sense that Wittgenstein asks about Shakespeare: 'Was he perhaps a *creator of language* rather than a poet?' (CV, p. 95). Even though he asks this question to highlight the distinctive greatness of Shakespeare, I argue that all poets are creators of language in the sense that they are creators of perspectives that bring readers to change their own perspectives, to find 'the right perspective', that is to find the perspective in which the poem makes sense for them.

Poets and artists give us new perspectives and only with their help can we realize that the ordinary is nothing ordinary, that, as Stanley Fish argues, at the heart of the ordinary lies the very possibility of the extraordinary; at the heart of our everyday language lies the possibility of literature and poetry (Fish 1982, 108). Artists are those who take this potentiality and make it actual as Nietzsche suggests:

> Only artists, and especially those of the theatre, have given men eyes and ears to see and hear with some pleasure what each man *is* himself, experiences himself, desires himself; only they have taught us to esteem the hero that is concealed in everyday characters; only they have taught us the art of viewing ourselves as heroes – from a distance and, as it were, simplified and transfigured – the art of staging and watching ourselves. Only in this way can we deal with some base details in ourselves. Without this art we would be nothing but the foreground and live entirely in the spell of that perspective which makes what is closest at hand and most vulgar appear as if it were vast, and reality itself. (GS 78 / KSA 3.433-4)

The artist's strength is to show us the extraordinary dwelling at the heart of the ordinary: we all are heroes, but we need the right perspective to realize it. This passage from GS is somehow similar to Wittgenstein's remark on theatre, but with a shift of focus from spectator to creator: whereas Wittgenstein draws our attention to the perspective one takes when looking at a stage, Nietzsche brings to light the way artists free us from the ordinary perspective according to which our surrounding world is reality itself. The last sentence, especially the idiom 'reality itself', might sound like it is bringing some metaphysical dimension back into the picture: the world of appearance is close to us, and reality is hidden behind it. However, I think there is something more subtle at play here: what Nietzsche is saying is that we need to take some distance from ourselves to understand that we are linked to a context or a situation which affects our understanding of ourselves. The 'reality' we perceive is always perspectival and situated; there is precisely no 'reality itself'.

In this sense, there are only the interpretations and the projections we make according to our situation and context. The idea of a 'true world' becomes inoperant because it is pragmatically useless: if there were, in a Kantian vocabulary, something like a 'thing in itself', we would not be able to reach it nor to ground our certainties in it. Whether it exists or not does not change anything to the way we perceive the world and situate ourselves within it. In that sense, metaphysics has been rendered useless and we need a different approach. This idea is the basis for Nietzsche's perspectivism:

> That mountain there! That cloud there! What is 'real' in that? Subtract the phantasm and every contribution from it, my sober friends! If you *can*! If you can forget your descent, our past, your training – all of your humanity and animality. There is no 'reality' for us – not for you either, my sober friends. (GS 57 / KSA 3.421-2)

Art allows us to take another perspective on our lives and ourselves and by doing so reveals new details. With this idea, as we have seen, Nietzsche's perspectivism moves from representationalism to expressivism. In this chapter, building on Wittgenstein's seeing-as/reading-as explored in the previous chapter, I discuss Nietzsche's perspectivism further, showing how a perspectival poetics brings to the fore a poetic world view and the poetics of philosophy. This chapter is divided into three parts: first, I move from the idea of perspectivism as an epistemological doctrine to a conception of an aesthetic perspectivism; second, I relate this aesthetic perspectivism to the question of values and the Nietzschean attempt at the revaluation of all values; third, I analyse the way in which this aesthetic perspectivism leads to a poetic world view.

1 Nietzsche, perspectivism, epistemology

In a very concise way, Arthur Danto defines perspectivism as 'the doctrine that there are no facts but only interpretations' (Danto 2005, 59). Despite its efficiency, this definition is not completely uncontestable. More specifically, whereas one part of this definition seems to be common sense to a Nietzschean discussion of perspectivism, another is subject to interpretation. The uncontested aspect of this definition is that perspectivism is about interpretation and suggests replacing the notion of fact by that of interpretation, that is, replacing the grounding of truth in an external and independent 'true world' by perspectives that are related to a subject's interpretations. As we have seen in previous chapters, this replacement is part of Nietzsche's critique of metaphysics and suggests that the interpreter is involved in the process of understanding the world and is not a mere passive and external observer. The contestable aspect of this definition is the idea that perspectivism is a doctrine. As already mentioned regarding Nietzsche's views on language, assigning any fixed and stable theory or doctrine to Nietzsche (as to Wittgenstein) is a dangerous move which misses the performative and rhetorical dimensions of his writings.

Without going as far as Werner Stegmaier who considers that Nietzsche's philosophy is not made of doctrines but only of signs indicating directions the reader can follow, attributing any kind of doctrine to Nietzsche can prove to be a contradictory task (Stegmaier 2006). This attribution is contradictory not only because his thinking evolves with time, and he reinterprets earlier works with later ideas – see, for example, the various prefaces written in 1886 – but also and above all because the fragmentary aesthetics of his works often presents aphorisms which contradict themselves if taken as elements of a doctrine. Because of the poetics of his philosophy, taking Nietzsche's ideas as doctrines only leads to the poetic paradox Zarathustra's disciple faces when Zarathustra claims that 'poets lie too much' while being himself a poet. The literary dimension of his writings calls for interpretation, and straightforward understandings of his aphorisms as building blocks for a doctrine leaves this aspect aside. A doctrine is always somehow absolute and tends towards universality whereas perspectivism states the opposite.

To elaborate my reading of Nietzsche's perspectivism as an 'aesthetic perspectivism', I proceed in two steps: in this section, I contest the idea that perspectivism is an epistemological doctrine and suggest that it rather offers an alternative to traditional epistemology; in the next section, I show the importance of value in perspectivism and argue that this importance of value is related to the aesthetic dimension of perspectivism.[2]

Many commentators in the English-speaking world consider perspectivism to be central to Nietzsche's philosophy and, more importantly, central to the use contemporary philosophy can make of Nietzsche.[3] According to Maudemarie Clark, Nietzsche's perspectivism 'constitutes his most obvious contribution to the current intellectual scene, the most widely accepted Nietzschean doctrine' (Clark 1990, 127). Clark's conception of Nietzsche's perspectivism relies on the idea that perspectivism is a matter of epistemology as she defines perspectivism as 'the claim that all knowledge is perspectival'. Although she points out that 'Nietzsche also characterizes values as perspectival', she is 'concerned here only with his perspectivism regarding knowledge' (Clark 1990, 127). Against Clark, I will explore the relation between perspectivism and values in the second part of this chapter.

Clark and the many scholars who agree on considering perspectivism an epistemological doctrine are confronted to the so-called self-refuting problem of perspectivism. To present this problem, Steven Hales and Rex Welshon oppose 'strong perspectivism' to 'absolutism':

> Recall that absolutism is the denial of strong perspectivism. Since strong perspectivism is the claim that every statement is true in some perspective and untrue in another, the following is a rendering of absolutism: there is at least one statement that is either true in all perspectives or untrue in all perspectives. [. . .] Suppose that strong perspectivism is true in all perspectives. If so, then there is a statement that has the same truth value in all perspectives – viz., the thesis of strong perspectivism itself. But, if there is some statement that has the same truth value in all perspectives, then absolutism is true, or, to put the matter in an equivalent form, if strong perspectivism is true in all perspectives, then strong perspectivism is untrue. (Hales and Welshon 2000, 22)

This treatment of Nietzsche's perspectivism is precisely what leads scholars to consider it to entail a contradiction. If we consider Hales and Welshon (and with them a certain tradition of Nietzsche interpretation) to be right in opposing perspectivism to absolutism, that is, as two opposed and distinct metaphysical–epistemological doctrines, then there is indeed a contradiction within Nietzsche's 'doctrine'. The next step for most commentators is then to find a way of avoiding this contradiction, for example, by proposing a 'weak perspectivism' in the case of Hales and Welshon or by showing that, despite his criticisms, Nietzsche has a minimal conception of truth as correspondence in the case of Clark.

The problem with these views is that they remain within the representationalist framework. We have seen that shifting to an expressivist conception of language frees us from the necessity of correspondence. Inasmuch as expressivism rejects the privilege given to representation by showing that it is only one language-game among others, Nietzsche's perspectivism rejects the privilege given to truth as correspondence by showing that it is only one kind of truth among many others. A more interesting move, and probably more consistent with Nietzsche's rhetoric, is therefore to consider perspectivism not as a doctrine opposed to absolutism but as an alternative way of thinking without doctrines. Doing so undercuts the contradiction as it moves perspectivism to another field of discussion. In other words, perspectivism would not be another epistemological doctrine, but an alternative to traditional epistemology. It would be, as Tracy Strong suggests, an attempt at replacing epistemology or, at least, at undermining the idea that epistemology must be representational (Strong 1985, 165).

Alan Schrift takes a first step towards this alternative by showing:

> Nietzsche's perspectival account does not provide a theory at all; it is a rhetorical strategy that offers an alternative to the traditional epistemological conception of knowledge as the possession of some stable, eternal 'entities,' whether these be considered 'truths,' 'facts,' 'meanings,' 'propositions,' or whatever. As we shall see, Nietzsche views these 'entities' as beyond the limits of human comprehension, and, whether or not they exist (a question Nietzsche regards as an 'idle hypothesis' [see WP, 560]), he concludes that we are surely incapable of 'knowing' them. (Schrift 1990, 145)

According to Schrift, Nietzsche's philosophy does not give us a theory of knowledge but, rather, explains why remaining within the metaphysical framework which considers world and words as *aeternae veritates* leads to the impossibility of knowledge. Translated in a Wittgensteinian framework, this idea suggests that the problem of scepticism is bound to the metaphysical/representational framework. Wittgenstein's move back to the ordinary is a move towards pragmatism that, as we have seen, Nietzsche also makes with his perspectivism.

Schrift's account of perspectivism brings us back to Danto's concise definition of it. Against the idea that there are facts (or any other stable metaphysical entity, a 'true world') of which we can reach an absolute knowledge, perspectivism suggests there are only interpretations that make up the world. This notion of interpretation casts an aesthetic or literary light on perspectivism, as Christoph Cox argues: 'Unlike the notion of "perspective" – which, literally construed, generates serious epistemological difficulties – the notion of "interpretation" operates within a rich and increasingly important literary and philosophical tradition' (Cox 1997, 272). The notion of interpretation interestingly brings to the fore the interpreter, the spectator, rather than what is seen, be it the 'world', 'reality', 'facts', notions which all have heavy metaphysical connotations. It is not really the notion of 'perspective' that generates difficulty but, rather, the placing of perspective in the representational framework of traditional epistemology.

Perspectivism offers an alternative to traditional epistemology insofar as it relies precisely on the interpreter, on the eye that sees rather than on the 'reality' which is seen. This dimension of vision, which is central to the notion of perspective itself, is however completely left aside in discussions on perspectivism. For instance, Hales' and Welshon's book-length discussion on perspectivism contains chapters on 'Truth', 'Logic', 'Ontology', 'Causality', Epistemology', 'Consciousness' and 'The Self' with almost no mention of perception at all.[4] In a sense, contemporary interpreters of Nietzsche remain within the traditional epistemological framework from which Nietzsche attempts to escape. The alternative to epistemology Nietzsche offers relies precisely on the notions of vision and perception. These notions are central to perspectivism, and we have seen that he considers the task of philosophy to be 'that of *viewing science through the optic of the artist, and art through the optic of life*' (BT 'Attempt' 2 / KSA 1.14).

Coming back to the etymology of aesthetics, *aisthesis*, sensation or perception, Nietzsche's focus on vision suggests that perspectivism should be linked to aesthetic concerns rather than epistemological ones. As Kathleen Higgins argues:

> This term [aesthetic] is appropriate, I think, because it gets at the root and range of the perspectival variables that are relevant to a true picture of the situations in which we apprehend. An additional advantage of the term is that Nietzsche's images drawn from the sphere of art and aesthetics more narrowly conceived usually reverberate, illuminating features of life, broadly conceived. Nietzsche dethrones 'traditional' epistemology from its queenly place in philosophy in favor of aesthetics, the study of perception and value within the perceptual sphere. (Higgins 2000, 52)

By bringing to the fore perception, and especially the place or situation of the perceiver, Nietzsche's perspectivism offers an alternative way to relate to the world, a way in which the seeing or perceiving is more fundamental than what is seen or perceived. Taken as a doctrine concerning knowledge, perspectivism is a self-refuting claim: if all is perspectival, then perspectivism is only a perspective. Nietzsche is well aware of this self-refuting problem, and we have seen that he responds to it in BGE only by saying 'then, all the better' (BGE 22 / KSA 5.37). Nietzsche's shift to a performative language in his reply to the charge of self-refutation suggests that the interpretation according to which perspectivism is self-refuting misses the central point. This claim is self-refuting only if one takes it as an epistemological or metaphysical doctrine, but perspectivism precisely aims at moving away from this epistemological–metaphysical framework. Returning to the etymological sense of aesthetics, perspectivism is an aesthetic matter, which places the perceptual and the sensual at the centre of philosophical concerns: perspectivism is a matter of perception and more precisely 'half visual experience half thought' (PPF 140) similar to Wittgenstein's 'seeing-as'.

Following Nietzsche, perspectivism would be an alternative to epistemology in a way similar to which aesthetics is an alternative to the rationalist philosophy of the sixteen and seventeenth centuries. Baumgarten's understanding of aesthetics as the science of sensations contests the rationalist's epistemology which relies solely on reason and suggests that the senses, too, can give us knowledge of the world. As Stefan Majetschak argues, Baumgarten's conception of aesthetics is a 'rebellion against the rationalist narrow concept of knowledge' (Majetschak 2007, 13). Nietzsche's perspectivism pursues Baumgarten's rehabilitation of the senses but takes it in a completely different direction. If there are no metaphysical entities we can know, the senses are not only a supplement to reason, but all that there is. A perspective, in this framework, could be considered a 'situated perception' or, in Wittgensteinian terms, a 'seeing-as'.

In this sense, Nietzsche operates the pragmatic shift Richard Rorty makes in criticizing philosophy as being the 'mirror of nature'. Against a representational epistemology and against a representational conception of language – which both rely on the metaphysical idea that the philosopher can objectively describe the world and that her being part of it does not influence the description – Nietzsche shifts the focus from the world and what we can say about it to the way we relate to it, to our perception, to our world view and to what we can do with it. Perspectivism shifts the focus from what one sees to how one sees and to the various elements (linguistic, cultural, moral, religious, historical, etc.) that modify the way of seeing. Nietzsche shifts from the representational idea that we can describe the world objectively to the expressivist idea that our relation to the world is always mediated by language (the metaphorical process in TL). As Nietzsche says: 'The way men usually are, it takes a name to make something visible for them' (GS 261, KSA 3.517).

This notion of seeing is also strongly present in one of the most famous of Nietzsche's texts on perspectivism in GM:

> From now on, my dear philosophers, let us beware of the dangerous old conceptual fable which posited a 'pure, will-less, painless, timeless knowing subject,' let us beware of the tentacles of such contradictory concepts as 'pure reason,' 'absolute spirituality,' 'knowledge in itself;' – for these always ask us to imagine an eye which is impossible to imagine, an eye which supposedly looks out in no particular direction, an eye which supposedly either restrains or altogether lacks the active powers of interpretation which first makes seeing into seeing something – for here, then, a nonsense and non-concept is demanded of the eye. Perspectival seeing is the *only* kind of seeing there is, perspectival 'knowing' the *only* kind of 'knowing;' and the *more* the feelings about a matter which we allow to come to expression, the *more* eyes, different eyes through which we are able to view this same matter, the more complete our 'conception' of it, our 'objectivity,' will be. (GM III 12/ KSA 5.365)

This passage condenses most of Nietzsche's critique of traditional modes of thinking and presents the main characteristics of his perspectivism. First of all, Nietzsche opposes the perspectival to the 'pure', the 'absolute' and the 'as such'. What Nietzsche criticizes here, as we have seen in the previous chapters, is the philosophical tendency to universalize a concept against the multiplicity of phenomena. Rather than stating his critique in terms of language and metaphysics as he does in TL, for instance, he elaborates it around the notion of 'seeing'. For any seeing to occur, there necessarily must be an eye, and therefore a subject, which perceives. Nietzsche criticizes philosophers who have tried to annihilate this subjectivity in order to reach absoluteness. He takes the counterpoint of his predecessors by promoting a perspectival seeing, that is, a seeing by an interpreting subject. It is interesting to note that Nietzsche first talks about a 'perspectival seeing' before a 'perspectival knowing'. Perspectivism is not at first a matter of knowledge but above all a matter of perception. If there is a perspectival knowing, it is only because in order to know something, one must first perceive it (and this often happens visually). This perception being perspectival, the knowledge built upon it can only be perspectival as well.

As already discussed in previous chapters, perspectivism does not lead to a radical relativism but to a conceptual one according to which we can never know what the world is outside of our conceptual scheme (or even if there is such a thing as 'the world') or, in a Nietzschean vocabulary, outside of our perspective. The perspective limits or frames the perception and therefore the knowledge elaborated from it. Perspectivism therefore mainly is an attack against the objectivity science or metaphysics pretend to reach. There cannot be any non-perspectival knowledge, and in opposition to the 'bad' objectivity he criticizes – objectivity which eradicates subjectivity – Nietzsche calls 'objectivity' the sum of the multiple perspectives. As the multiplicity of perspectives is, if not infinite, at least indefinite, one can never reach any absolute sum, any absolute objectivity. The knowledge of a thing depends first on our perspectival seeing, then on our description of it. And one element essential to any description of a thing is, according to Nietzsche, the affects we put into our words: the more affects, the better the description.

2 The values of perspectivism

The idea of affects brings to the fore the connection between perspectivism and values that Nietzsche suggests in his 1886 'Attempt at a Self-Criticism' in BT. In this retrospective account, Nietzsche links perspectivism to the revaluation of all values. More than a connection aiming at conceptualizing his early work, we could say that the revaluation of all values calls for a change of perspective. This connection is a hint towards considering perspectivism on the grounds of values rather than knowledge. Knowledge, for Nietzsche, should not necessarily be valued positively. He does not cast doubts on knowledge itself, but on the value we give it, on our taking knowledge as the most important (if not the only possible) perspective. In other words, traditional epistemology is only one perspective among others. Perspectivism is therefore not another epistemological doctrine but operates at a more fundamental level of conceptualizing our relation to the world. By taking perspectivism as an aesthetic and axiological matter rather than an epistemological one, we can come to a more convincing use of the notion. Perspectivism is above all a matter of vision and seeing, of the way we relate to the world, and by taking this notion back to its original ground of perception, we cannot only connect it to Wittgenstein's 'seeing-as' but also to Nietzsche's early conceptions of language and metaphors.

Nietzsche's perspectivism aims to show that there can be no knowledge without context, no absolute knowledge, for there is no 'objective' perception. All perception is perspectival and linked to a perceiving subject. Whereas Wittgenstein's focus with 'seeing-as' is on the object seen, Nietzsche's perspectivism focuses on who does the seeing. 'Seeing-as' and perspectivism both revolve around the same idea – 'seeing-as' is a kind of perspectivism – but the former focuses on what is seen and the possible interpretations, whereas the latter focuses on who or what sees and the affects at play in this perspectival seeing. The main difference between Nietzsche and Wittgenstein is that Nietzsche takes perspectivism into the realm of values, therefore linking it to his critiques of morality and culture, whereas Wittgenstein's main focus with 'seeing-as' is not culture but psychology. Of course, psychology is important for Nietzsche as well – he considers psychology as the 'queen of the sciences' (BGE 23 / KSA 5.39) – but Nietzsche and Wittgenstein do not operate at the same level: Wittgenstein seeks to observe and describe the effects of psychology on seeing, among other things, whereas Nietzsche focuses on the deeper and unconscious level of the influence of affects and context on psychology. Their shared concern with psychology does, however, lead them to connect seeing to interpreting, and therefore to language.

Perspectival seeing can already be seen as playing a role in Nietzsche's conception of language in TL. Whereas most commentators take TL to contain an early version of perspectivism in which Nietzsche has not yet abandoned the thing-in-itself, I believe that we can interpret Nietzsche's notion of metaphor as a perspectival seeing. Most of the critiques regarding Nietzsche's perspectivism in TL concern its focus on the thing-in-itself, the object of perspectivism (Conant 2005, 40–9). This focus forces Nietzsche to hold a difficult metaphysical position in which he criticizes truth as correspondence, metaphysical language and the thing-in-itself, while using them to say what he wants. If we shift focus from the object to the subject, as Nietzsche does in his later works, there are quite a few elements which can be of use to perspectivism in TL.

The main element I will focus on is the notion of metaphor which is the place of the perspectival seeing. Indeed, Nietzsche describes language as being the result of a double metaphorical process: 'To begin with, a nerve stimulus is transferred into an image: first metaphor. The image, in turn, is imitated into a sound: second metaphor' (TL 1 / KSA 1.879). In this sense, metaphor operates a translation and we must shift our focus from the thing (the sense data) to the perspective. If there is a translation, this means it is a process and that elements from the context (external and internal to the perceiver) can come into play. The seeing process characterized as metaphor can therefore be understood as a 'seeing-as' or an interpretation. This is Sarah Kofman's thesis mentioned in Chapter 1 according to which Nietzsche replaces metaphor with perspective and interpretation in his later works (Kofman 1993, 82). The process Nietzsche describes concerns various metaphorical processes: the translation from stimuli to images is only the first one. The second metaphor gets closer to Wittgenstein's 'seeing-as': the image created in the perceiver's mind is then translated into a word. The perceiver does therefore not yet understand the images: understanding calls for another metaphorical process. The image is interpreted through its translation into a word. We have seen that, for Wittgenstein, interpretation does not always play a role in 'seeing-as'. In the Nietzschean process, it would mean that the translation from image to word is sometimes immediate, without reflection, sometimes requires interpretation. As Nietzsche's theory aims at explaining the origins of language, it would mean that language is built on various 'seeing-as' and that new language can be created with new 'seeing-as', new perspectives.

What happens between the 'seeing' and the 'seeing-as'? What happens between the first and the second metaphor? Whether there is a conscious interpretative process or not, a whole set of values is brought into the seeing. When observing, the perceiver brings her whole system of values with her. And language is filled with values: 'Every word is a prejudice' (WS 55 / KSA 2.577), Nietzsche argues, and every value judgement is a perspective:

> You must learn how to grasp the perspectival element in every valuation – the displacement, distortion, and seeming teleology of horizons and everything else that pertains to perspectivism; and also how much stupidity there is in opposed values and the whole intellectual loss that must be paid for every For, every Against. You must learn to grasp the necessary injustice in every For and Against, injustice as inseparable from life, life itself as conditioned by perspective and its injustice. (HH 'Preface' 6 / KSA 2. 20)

In this passage, Nietzsche explicitly relates perspectivism to values. Knowledge is perspectival in the sense that knowledge is a perspective taken on life, and it is not the only perspective. With each perspective comes a value judgement, and Nietzsche uses perspectivism to show that what we usually take for granted are only perspectives and that what we take for being good or bad is only a value attached to such a perspective. The opposition between true and untrue is a perspective (or an optics) through which we look at the world. In this perspective, we attribute positive values to truth, negative ones to lies. However, and hence the title 'On Truth and Lie in a *Non-Moral Sense*', other perspectives can be taken, with other valuations attached to them.

This casting doubts on the value we attribute to truth is the starting point of BGE: as there is no such thing as an objective, real or absolutely true perspective, our valuations must depend on other criteria, be it beauty, use, love and so on. As much as the description depends on the describing subject, the valuation depends on the evaluating subject. Perspectives and valuations are numerous, and one can change perspective at any time (just as one can focus on the duck or the rabbit in Wittgenstein's duck-rabbit example). This does not mean that changing perspective is something easy to do; on the contrary, it is rather difficult and violent as one has to abandon one's old ways of seeing.[5] Because of their unconstrained imagination and their supposedly innocent gaze, children (and they are an example Wittgenstein also uses a lot) are great at changing perspectives. And let us not forget that 'In a genuine man a child is hidden: it wants to play' (TSZ I 'Women' / KSA 4.85). The image of the child is a recurring feature in Nietzsche's philosophy and especially in TSZ. Let us not forget that the child is the last transformation of the spirit after the camel and the lion. The child is the yes-saying spirit: 'the spirit now wills *its own* will, the one who had lost the world attains *its own* world' (TSZ I 'Transformations' / KSA 4.31). The spirit transformed back into a child is the only one that can affirm the world and affirm its own world. It is the spirit that can affirm its own perspectives. Whereas the camel follows the established perspectives and collapses under the weight of old values, whereas the lion negates the old values with a negative or destructive perspective, the child is the one who can create from the debris of the old values, who can affirm positive and creative perspectives.

Following one of Heraclitus' images, Nietzsche compares the poet to the child at play. This child, according to Nietzsche's reading of Heraclitus, playfully destroys and creates perspectives.

> That striving towards the infinite, the beating of the wings of longing, which accompanies the highest joy in clearly perceived reality, recall that we must recognize in both states a Dionysian phenomenon, which reveals to us again and again the playful construction and destruction of the individual world as the overflow of an original joy, in a similar way to that in which Heraclitus the Obscure compares the world-forming force to a child at play, arranging and scattering stones here and there, building and then trampling sand-hills. (BT 24 / KSA 1.153)

This child at play, this yes-saying spirit destroying and creating perspectives, is similar to the poet who offers an aesthetic interpretation of the world.[6] The Dionysian poet, too, creates and destroys perspectives to give her interpretation of the world. At the opposite of this aesthetic interpretation is the moral one Christianity defends:

> In truth, there is no greater contradiction of the purely aesthetic interpretation and justification of the world as it is taught in this book than the Christian doctrine which is and wants to be exclusively moral and, with its absolute standard – already for example with the truthfulness of God – exiles art, *each and every* art, to the realm of *lies* – that is, denies, damns, condemns it. (BT 'Attempt' 5 / KSA 1.18)

The moral perspective is opposed to the aesthetic one because the former aims at stability whereas the latter aims at movement. There are many interpretations of the world: art and religion are two perspectives (and even more as art and religion contain many different perspectives). What Nietzsche criticizes in Christianity and the herd morality is its claim to be the unique interpretation of the world.

Nietzsche criticizes science on similar grounds: 'A "scientific" interpretation of the world, as you understand it, might therefore still be one of the *most stupid* of all possible interpretations of the world, meaning that it would be one of the poorest in meaning' (GS 373 / KSA 3.626). Science is only one interpretation among others, and by taking it as the 'true' interpretation, we follow the mistakes of metaphysical absoluteness. More than science itself, Nietzsche criticizes scientism, the application of scientific method to all objects. Interpreting the world (and this means not only the natural world but also the cultural one) according to the sole perspective of scientific method precisely reduces the number of perspectives to a single one. Hence scientism would be the poorest in meaning because it is the poorest in the number of possible perspectives whereas the poetic allows for multiple perspectives to coexist. And the poetic is necessary to human life, as Rorty argues:

> The fear of science, of 'scientism,' of 'naturalism,' of self-objectivation, of being turned by too much knowledge into a thing rather than a person, is the fear that all discourse will become normal discourse. That is, it is the fear that there will be objectively true or false answers to every question we ask, so that human worth will consist in knowing truths, and human virtue will be merely justified true belief. This is frightening because it cuts off the possibility of something new under the sun, of human life as poetic rather than merely contemplative. (Rorty 2009, 388–9)

Scientism is, however, not the only danger according to Nietzsche; a similar critique can be made to metaphysics and religion, especially Christianity as we have seen. This opposition between the plurality of perspectives and the single one promoted by Christianity can be linked to Nietzsche's conception of 'eternal recurrence': eternal recurrence could be interpreted as the neverending process of destroying and creating perspectives, whereas Christianity promotes a motionless eternity: eternal life is perhaps the most contradictory conception insofar as life is nothing but movement. The eternal recurrence is opposed to eternal life as movement is opposed to stability. Morality and science work towards constructing their 'cyclopic building' (GS 7 / KSA 3.380), towards establishing their single perspective. But as Nietzsche often argues, and his critiques of morality and science occur on the same grounds as those of metaphysics and religion, to identify everything under a single perspective loses the multiplicity of life: 'Behind such a way of thinking and evaluating, which must be hostile to art, if it is at all genuine, I always sensed *hostility to life*, the wrathful and vengeful disgust at life itself: for all life is founded on appearance, art, illusion, optic, the necessity of the perspectival and of error' (BT 'Attempt' 5 / KSA 1.18).

Religion, scientism and morality are hostile to life, and Nietzsche considers them nihilistic. To remain enclosed within one perspective is nihilistic as it contradicts the multiplicity of life. Indeed, existence is full of different perspectives giving various meanings (and this to an indefinite extent):

> How far the perspective character of existence extends or indeed whether existence has any other character than this; whether existence without interpretation, without 'sense,' does not become 'nonsense'; whether, on the

other hand, all existence is not essentially engaged in *interpretation* – that cannot be decided even by the most industrious and most scrupulously conscientious analysis and self-examination of the intellect; for in the course of this analysis the human intellect cannot avoid seeing itself in its own perspectives, and *only* in these. [. . .] Rather has the world become 'infinite' for us all over again, inasmuch as we cannot reject the possibility that *it may include infinite interpretations*. (GS 374 / KSA 3.626-7)

Poetry and art might therefore be better at describing existence than science or religion because they allow for the multiplicity of perspectives to exist and coexist. This is precisely Nietzsche's and Wittgenstein's move against metaphysics, against the idea that the world can be fully grasped from one unique and only perspective. Rorty describes the quarrel between philosophy and poetry in these opposing terms of unicity and multiplicity: 'To take the side of the poets in this quarrel is to say that there are many descriptions of the same things and events, and that there is no neutral standpoint from which to judge the superiority of one description over another. Philosophy stands in opposition to poetry just insofar as it insists that there is such a standpoint' (Rorty 2016, 20). While a philosophical world view aims at reaching the essence of things, the ultimate description, a poetic world view accepts that there are many possible descriptions that all have a certain value.

3 A poetic world view

Wreckage of stars:
I built a world from this wreckage
Nietzsche, *'Through the circle of Dionysos Dithyrambs'*

(Nietzsche 2010, 323)

Perspectivism is both an aesthetic and poetic matter: it is an aesthetic one because it is based on the multiplicity of perceptions through which we relate to the world; it is a poetic matter because the perspectives, following the etymology of poetry, *poiesis*, are made or created. The multiplicity of perspectives and interpretations leads to various poetic world views created by a subject, the 'eye' (and hence the 'I') which is always at the source of the seeing as Nietzsche argues. If a world view is poetic, it is because it is created, made, crafted. A perspectival poetics means a making of perspectives which leads to a poetic world view.

In such a poetic world view 'What I want is more; I am no seeker. I want to create myself a sun of my own' (GS 320 / KSA 3.320). Against the Platonic idea that there is a sun that objectively enlightens everything for subjects to see, in the world view of perspectivism the subject creates her own sun, her own perspective. She must abandon the passive descriptive stance and become a creator of perspectives:

> Moving away from things until there is a good deal that one no longer sees and there is much that our eye has to add if we are still to see them at all; or seeing things around a corner and as cut out and framed; or to place them so that they partially conceal each other and grant us only glimpses of architectural perspectives; or looking at them through tinted glass or in the light of the sunset; or giving them a surface and skin that is not fully transparent – all this we should learn from artists while being wiser than they are in other matters. For with them this subtle power usually comes to an end where art and life begins; but we want to be poets of our life – first of all in the smallest, most everyday matters. (GS 299 / KSA 3.538)

To be poets of our life means to be creators of our life because, as in Apollinaire's description of the task of poetry, 'It is that poetry and creation are one and the same; only that man can be called poet who invents, who creates insofar as man can create. The poet is who discovers new joys, even if they are hard to bear. One can be a poet in any field: it is enough that one be adventuresome and pursue new discovery' (Cook 2004, 80). Just as the artist's perspective reveals the hero within us, we can adopt the right perspective to become poets and heroes of our life, creators of something rather than followers. In this sense, creation is Nietzsche's escape route from herd morality. But how can one become a creator?

According to Nietzsche the act of creation is tightly linked to the act of destruction: to create one must destroy. And one way of creating things for the poet is to create words:

> to realize that what things *are called* is incomparably more important than what they are. [...] What at first was appearance becomes in the end, almost invariably, the essence and is effective as such. How foolish it would be to suppose that one only needs to point out this origin and this misty shroud of delusion in order to *destroy* the world that counts for real, so-called

'*reality*'. We can destroy only as creators. – But let us not forget this either: it is enough to create new names and estimations and probabilities in order to create in the long run new 'things'. (GS 58 / KSA 3.422)

In order to destroy the false belief in the metaphysical dualism between reality and appearance, the philosopher must create 'new things' to replace the 'old' ones. The creation of something new replaces the old one and therefore destroys it. In order to create these 'new things', one must create new words to account for those not yet existing things. This calls for originality according to Nietzsche: 'What is originality? *To see* something that has no name yet and hence cannot be mentioned although it stares us all in the face. The way men usually are, it takes a name to make something visible for them. – Those with originality have for the most part also assigned names' (GS 261 / KSA 3.261). In order to create new words, one needs originality and an original perspective. The word is the product of a certain perspective and the creation of a word creates possibilities of interpretation. In turn, this new word allows new perspectives to be taken on the world. The process is therefore double: a perspective creates a new word and a new word creates new possibilities in interpretation, that is, new perspectives.

We must not forget that interpretation is not always conscious; it can happen unconsciously (and often does, as with Wittgenstein's seeing-as). This notion of unconscious which Nietzsche elaborates quite extensively is another aspect of the critique of metaphysics and its 'magic' language as the metaphysical conceptions of language and the world are made by negating the unconscious:

> This is the essence of phenomenalism and perspectivism as *I* understand them: Owing to the nature of *animal consciousness*, the world of which we can become conscious is only a surface- and a sign-world, a world that is made common and meaner; whatever becomes conscious *becomes* by the same token shallow, thin, relatively stupid, general, sign, herd, signal; all becoming conscious involves a great art and thorough corruption, falsification, reduction to superficialities, and generalization. (GS 354 / KSA 3.593)

This process of 'becoming conscious' is what happens in the metaphorical transposition of an image into a word: we become conscious of the object through the word. But the world disclosed through this process of naming loses its uniqueness: words equate unequal metaphors. There is a whole world of which we are not conscious either because it is lost in the process of naming or has not been named yet. And this unconscious dimension of the world is not the least part of it. To some extent, Nietzsche's unconscious world is similar to Wittgenstein's 'mystical'. The unconscious is what cannot be named because there is no word to describe it yet.

What a perspectival poetics teaches us is that a poetic world view calls for destruction and creation or, better, destruction through creation and vice versa. This is a point on which Nietzsche's and Wittgenstein's views seem the most distant from one another as Wittgenstein considers that philosophy should remain at the level of description. However, description can lead to change as it can lead to take another perspective on a matter and might even require the creation of a perspective which can satisfy the description, in the same sense that one might need to create a context to understand a sign. As Alexander Nehamas suggests, any new interpretation is a reinterpretation:

> As in the literary case, so in the world, according to Nietzsche, to reinterpret events is to rearrange effects and therefore to generate new things. Our 'text' is being composed as we read it, and our readings are new parts of it that will give rise to further ones in the future. Even the reinterpretation of existing formulas adds to the world, especially since Nietzsche often thinks of interpretation as 'the introduction of meaning – not "explanation" (in most cases a new interpretation over an old interpretation that has become incomprehensible, that is now itself only a sing)' (*WP*, 604). To introduce new interpretations, therefore, it is necessary to reinterpret old ones. (Nehamas 1985, 91)

In this process of reinterpretation, the old interpretation disappears. Nietzsche's process of creation of perspectives destroys the one-sided perspective we usually follow. We must overcome the absoluteness of the scientific, moral and religious (those being linked for Nietzsche) perspectives to embrace the plurality of perspectives without privileging one or another *a priori*. Nietzsche does not want science, morality and religion to disappear, but he wants to escape their absolute character. Science, morality or Christianity cannot be the highest goal, for there is no highest goal. It is, however, clear that if the scientific perspective loses its absoluteness, it will not be the same perspective as the one we know (perhaps it will become the wisdom perspective from Greek culture); and the same goes for the herd morality and Christianity. The overcoming of the old perspectives should not be seen as a Hegelian '*Aufhebung*' because it is not the opposition of two perspectives that gives rise to a third uniting one but, as Nietzsche suggests with his conception of fight between wills to power, the constant fight between perspectives that lead to consider perspectivism as the only viable option. Nietzsche's interest is in the fight itself, not the issue (for there is no issue). Various interpretations fight against each other in what Paul Ricoeur calls the 'conflict of interpretations' (Ricoeur 2007). One of these fights between perspectives can be exemplified by the 'quarrel' between philosophy and poetry, two interpretations which enrich one another.

To exemplify this overcoming of old perspectives through the fight with new perspectives, both Nietzsche and Wittgenstein use the figure of the child. The poetic world view could very well be called a childlike world view, in a positive sense. We have seen that, in TSZ, the third and final transformation of the spirit is in the yes-saying child, and that Wittgenstein calls for the children's imagination in order to discuss the notion of 'seeing-as'. Wittgenstein's example shows that one cannot sustain multiple interpretations at the same time: the children see the chest as a house and no longer as a chest, just as it is not possible to see both the duck and the rabbit at the same time but only to shift from one to another. In their games, children use a different perspective and enrich the usual one. The poet, or the artist in general, has something of a child (or has preserved a childish character), and poetry or other arts all play a role in creating world views which we can follow or not. Using a different terminology, Nelson Goodman considers 'that the arts must be taken no less seriously than the sciences as modes of discovery, creation, and enlargement of knowledge in the broad sense of advancement of the understanding, and thus that the philosophy of art should be conceived as an integral part of metaphysics and epistemology' (Goodman 1995, 102). Whereas I agree with Goodman that the arts should be given an importance similar to that of the sciences, I think perspectivism overcomes the distinction between philosophy of art, metaphysics and epistemology. Once taken into account, perspectivism states that they are all perspectives to which we give more or less importance. With the rise and progress of science, epistemology has become the valuable perspective. But let us not forget that the multiplicity of perspectives will always be more valuable than a single one, for a problem in a perspective might be solved by shifting point of view. This is, once again, one of the reasons Nietzsche criticizes science as a 'cyclopic building' whose single eye cannot account for the depth of the world. The creation of new perspectives is a way to give depth to the world. To give depth to the world is also to give depth to our lives, as mentioned before, 'we want to be poets of our life'. Why should one limit oneself to seeing only the duck in the duck-rabbit? And why should one limit oneself to viewing the world as science presents it? There are many ways of approaching and making the world, and there are no reasons other than sociocultural norms to explain why we give privilege to one over another.

We have seen that Nietzsche criticizes scientism and religion as nihilistic perspectives which enclose within one perspective only. On the contrary, poetry – and art in general – represents a lively perspective, one in which one can live. Heidegger argues towards something similar in 'Poetically Man Dwells': 'Poetry is what really lets us dwell. But through what do we attain to a dwelling place? Through building. Poetic creation, which lets us dwell, is a kind of building' (Heidegger 2013, 213). For Heidegger, poetry understood as *poiesis* is a making, creating, building of a world in which we can live. It is an attempt at making sense of the world, a perspective from which things can make sense. If, following Nietzsche's 'death of God', there is no given meaning to existence and that nihilistic perspectives should be avoided, poetry and art offer an element of an answer. In this perspective-building, poetry reveals something of our relation to the world which, like the language we use to describe it, does never exist out of a perspectival viewing. And when this perspectival viewing comes to one's consciousness, one realizes that all seeing is not only a 'seeing-as' (intentional or not) but also a creating of such a 'seeing-as'. To that extent, poetry *qua poiesis* shares quite a lot with philosophy as they both engage in the activity of creating perspectives.

Philosophy and poetry share the idea that a world view or a perspective has a poetics: every perspective is created. Poetry, but to a wider extent art, is the place where this perspectival poetics reveals itself as such, as the creation of a world view. If the task of philosophy is to uncover this perspectival poetics and bring it to one's consciousness, it overlaps the task of poetry and the arts. Once philosophy abandons the idea of metaphysics and adopts the multiplicity of perspectives as an essential feature of our relation to the world, it must find a way of expressing it. Insights can be found in poetry and other arts, but, in the end, this means that a perspectival poetics leads to the poetics of philosophy.

Conclusion

A poetic philosophy of language

Poetry is a challenge to and a limit for a representational philosophy of language. If we are not to make the Platonic move of banishing poetry from the realm of language, an alternative is required. This alternative can be found in a specific form of expressivism, which I have called *Poetic Expressivism* and that builds on the works of Nietzsche and Wittgenstein, situating them within the larger framework of German *Romantic Expressivism* and contemporary *Pragmatic Expressivism*. This *Poetic Expressivism* constructs a poetic philosophy of language, in the sense that it is not merely a study of poetic language, but an investigation of how the poetic lies within language and of how poetry dwells within philosophy. Rather than identifying or categorizing philosophy as poetry, following the Romantic enterprise, Nietzsche claims that philosophy can be enriched from poetry. This goes against the idea of a generic difference between philosophy and poetry and, following this line of thought, Manfred Frank 'contends that literary discourse does not differ in either principle or quality, but merely *quantitatively*, from other innovative uses of colloquial language. Creative literature (*Dichtung*) is merely the extreme form of the innovative potential found in our everyday use of language' (Frank 1999, 275). Poetry uses the innovative possibilities of our language to its maximal capacity according to Frank, but philosophy can use them as well. By turning to a poetic style in the etymological sense of *poiesis*, philosophy acquires a creative dimension.

An important aspect of this creative use of language in philosophy is its focus on expression, in contrast to representation. Nietzsche's metaphors of laughter and dance in TSZ and other of his works are good illustrations of this shift to expression. For Nietzsche, dance is a metaphor for an expressive language and brings to the fore the bodily dimension of writing and reading.[1] Similarly, laughter has a bodily dimension and represents an expressive burst. Dance and laughter are two modes of expression that Nietzsche uses as metaphors. A third one appears quite often as well: singing. In his 'Attempt at self-criticism', Nietzsche criticizes his own style, considering that 'It should have *sung*, this "new soul" – rather than spoken!' (BT 'Attempt' 3 / KSA 1.15). In the shorter version from TSZ: 'Sing! Speak no more!' (TSZ III 'Seals' 7 / KSA 4.291). This opposition between speaking and singing reflects the opposition between prose and poetry. Songs belong to the realm of poetry, and Nietzsche often inscribes his works in poetic traditions. For instance, GS is subtitled 'la gaya scienza' thus referring to the Provençal art of troubadours and is followed by an appendix of songs. With this focus on dance, song and poetry, the notion of rhythm comes to the fore, as we have seen with Nietzsche's and Wittgenstein's remarks on poetry. In HH, Nietzsche claims: '*Thoughts in poems.* – The poet leads his thoughts along festively, upon the chariot of rhythm: usually because they cannot walk on their own feet' (HH 189 / KSA 2.164). If thoughts in poetry cannot walk, does this mean they can dance? The idea of a bodily expression comes back as a metaphor for the poetics of philosophy.

This idea of expression, especially in relation to music, can also be found in Wittgenstein who considers his style to be 'bad musical composition' (CV, p. 45). Although it is *bad* musical composition, it is musical nonetheless, and Wittgenstein acknowledges the importance of the expressive dimension in the writing of philosophy. According to Marjorie Perloff, his attention to the choice of words make him some kind of poet: 'Or perhaps the "uniqueness" in our postromantic age is less a matter of authenticity of individual *expression* than of sensitivity to the language pool on which the poet draws in re-creating and redefining the world as he or she has found it. It is in this context that Wittgenstein himself can be considered a poet' (Perloff 1996, 187). More than a being poet, Wittgenstein acknowledges the potential of poetry for philosophy:

> I believe I summed up where I stand in relation to philosophy when I said: really one should write philosophy only as one writes a poem. That, it seems to me, must reveal how far my thinking belongs to the present, the future, or the past. For I was acknowledging myself, with these words, to be someone who cannot quite do what he would like to be able to do. (CV, p. 28)

Wittgenstein does not claim that philosophy and poetry are one and the same, but that philosophy can gain from being written like one writes a poem, with a specific concern with words and language. It is this attention to language that the philosopher must take from the poet. Wittgenstein, however, acknowledges that he 'cannot quite do what he would like to be able to do' insofar as his style is perhaps not poetic enough. Both Nietzsche and Wittgenstein therefore acknowledge the idea that their language has not yet reached their ideal, but this is also perhaps because such an ideal cannot be reached. Indeed, if poetry points out what still needs to be done, what still needs to be created, it must be seen as representing the future, as an aim towards which Wittgenstein – and philosophy – must strive. Philosophy should be like poetry in the sense that it should always look forward, look towards using the creative powers at its disposal. Hence can we understand the middle sentence of Wittgenstein's remark that is often overlooked. His thinking belongs not only to the past and the present but also to the future. In its encounter with poetry, philosophy becomes concerned with the future. Traditional philosophies of language, following the opening lines of Julia Kristeva's *Revolution in Poetic Language*, are 'embodiments of the Idea, are nothing more than the thoughts of archivists, archaeologists, and necrophiliacs' (Kristeva 1984, 13). The notion of idea brings back the problem of metaphysics and is now related to a temporal dimension: a metaphysical philosophy of language is the work of archivists and necrophiliacs. Against this idea, a philosophy of language of the future must detach itself from metaphysics and from the past and one way to do it is to embrace poetry.

In this sense, a poetic philosophy of language is what Nietzsche calls a philosophy of the future, which creates new perspectives and values. The following quote from BGE insists on the creative dimension of a perspectivist philosophy of the future:

> I must insist that we finally stop mistaking philosophical workers or learned people in general for philosophers – in this regard especially, we should give strictly 'to each his own,' and not too much to the former or too little to the latter. The education of the true philosopher may require that he himself once pass through all the stages at which his servants, the learned workers of philosophy, remain – *must* remain. Perhaps he even needs to have been a critic and a sceptic and a dogmatic and an historian, and in addition a poet and collector and traveller and puzzle-solver and moralist and seer and 'free spirit' and nearly all things, so that he can traverse the range of human values and value-feelings and *be able* to look with many kinds of eyes and consciences from the corners into every wide expanse. But all these are only

the preconditions for his task: the task itself calls for something else – it calls for him to *create values*. It is the task of those philosophical workers in the noble mould of Kant and Hegel to establish and press into formulae some large body of value judgments (that is, previous value-*assumptions*, value-creations that have become dominant and are for a time called 'truths'), whether in the realm of *logic* or of *politics* (morals) or of *aesthetics*. [. . .] *But true philosophers are commanders and lawgivers*. They say, 'This is the way it should be!' Only they decide about mankind's Where to? and What for? and to do so they employ the preparatory work of all philosophical workers, all subduers of the past. With creative hands they reach towards the future, and everything that is or has existed becomes their means, their tool, their hammer. Their 'knowing' is creating, their creating is law-giving, their will to truth is – will to power. (BGE 211 / KSA 5.144-5)

There are many elements at play in this famous text, and I will point out three that outline the creative task in Nietzsche's philosophy.

1. The task of the philosopher is once again compared to that of the poet, although not exclusively. The philosopher needs to have been a poet among many other things, 'nearly all things' Nietzsche says. To become a philosopher of the future, one must go through many stages, and one of them is the poetic stage. This necessity to go through many stages parallels the idea that one should experience as many perspectives as possible in order to reach a better and more 'objective' understanding of a thing, to reach what Wittgenstein calls a 'surveyable representation [*übersichtliche Darstellung*]' (PI 122). The philosopher must 'traverse the range of human values and value-feelings and *be able* to look with many kinds of eyes and consciences from the corners into every wide expanse'. The philosopher must, one could say, have a perspectivist education and multiply the directions in which she looks. Without this moving through perspectives, the philosopher remains a mere philosophical worker, a 'subduer of the past'. Even though Nietzsche acknowledges the importance of such workers, they are not philosophers of the future, they are no creators.

2. In contrast to the single-mindedness of philosophical workers, the multiplicity of perspectives and stages the philosopher of the future must go through are preliminary steps for the philosopher's real task which is 'to *create values*'. This creation of values is the necessary stage for the

philosopher to endorse her role, that of a commander and a law-giver. To create new perspectives on the world, the philosopher follows the poet in creating a new language which, in turn, creates new things. These new things, that is this new conception of the world, lead the philosopher to create new values. This work builds on 'the preparatory works of all philosophical workers, subduers of the past'. Nietzsche uses temporal notions to classify philosophers: philosophical workers are concerned with the past whereas creative philosophers are philosophers of the future. This can be linked to Wittgenstein's concern with his own philosophy when discussing the idea that philosophy should be written as a poem. We have interpreted this idea by affirming that the task of poetry within philosophy or, better, the impact of poetry on philosophy, is to make philosophy look towards the future. The same goes for Nietzsche who considers that it is the philosopher's creative – or poetic – powers that characterize the philosopher of the future.

3. The philosopher of the future's 'knowing is creating'. All that has been called truths are, ultimately, creations, fictions, inventions which have become dominant: the fictions upon which the people have agreed (pragmatically or dogmatically). However, the task of the philosopher of the future is to overcome these dominant truths (and that is the step Nietzsche attempts to make by showing that these truths are constructions or fictions) and to propose new truths by creating new values. For Nietzsche, metaphysics can be criticized from the standpoint that it establishes a system of values which consider truth as the absolute and ultimate value. On the contrary, his perspectival vocabulary suggests that one should not remain enclosed within one system of values, but rather acknowledge the perspectival and thus relative dimension of our values. The task of the philosopher of the future is thus to uncover the perspectival dimension of values and undermine the metaphysical system. Hence Nietzsche's use of the hammer as philosophical tool: it can break, build, and, as in TI, sound out the idols. The sounding out of the idols reveals that they are empty, thus revealing the emptiness of all metaphysical systems. The task then remains of rebuilding, of creating. For Nietzsche, the value we give to truth is related to a question of power and hierarchy. The revaluation of values aims at revaluating this hierarchy without establishing a new

system, because this would just be repeating what Nietzsche criticizes. The revaluation of values has no end; it is a never-ending process, and this might be one way of reading the eternal recurrence. The last sentence from the quote suggests a process: knowing is creating, creating is law-giving, will to truth is will to power. The passage from law-giving to will to truth can be understood in the sense that truth justifies the law, and this in turn must be seen as a power justification. This process must, however, not have an end and the philosopher of the future always engages in this process of creating.

The philosopher, once she has encountered and experienced the poetic perspective, becomes not only a knower but a creator and a law-giver whose creations become new perspectives from which to look at the world. While Nietzsche clearly embraces this creative dimension in philosophy, how does Wittgenstein fit into this picture? Isn't Wittgenstein's idea that the task of philosophy is to 'leave everything as it is?' (PI 124). A straightforward reading would consider him to be completely opposed to the creative dimension of Nietzsche's philosophy. However, Wittgenstein's philosophy also has a creative dimension, which is to be found in the idea of invention. He does not only describe uses of language (i.e. the past) but also invents new ones (i.e. the future), as he argues in the *Blue Book*: 'That is also why our method is not merely to enumerate actual usages of words, but rather deliberately to invent new ones, some of them because of their absurd appearance' (BB, p. 28). With this focus on invention, Wittgenstein uses the poetic powers of language in order to transform the world and our understanding of it.

In this sense, the opposition between creation and description, between a straightforward reading of Nietzsche and a straightforward reading of Wittgenstein, reflects an uncritical reading of the analytic – continental divide. This divide is a misunderstanding rather than an absolute truth, just as the opposition between creation and description is. They are two sides of the same coin that lead to the therapeutic or transformative activity of philosophy.[2] This transformative dimension is not limited to continental philosophy, as Critchley seems to suggest,[3] insofar as even a description can have a therapeutic – and thus transformative – dimension. This transformative dimension can therefore not serve as dividing between two sides but, to the contrary, functions as a bridging notion.

Once analytic philosophers take into account the poetic aspects of language, as Wittgenstein for instance does, and continental philosophers the necessary communicative and normative aspects of language, as Nietzsche suggests it already, the differences seem to vanish. The confrontation with poetry brings Nietzsche and Wittgenstein not only to elaborate views on language which combine aspects from representational and expressive conceptions of language but also to adopt a specific style which can be characterized as poetic. Rather than considering analytic and continental philosophy as two traditions which are completely distinct from one another – and we have seen that neither can be ultimately defined – they can be considered as perspectives or sets of perspectives, which, as with all perspectives, require work to shift from one to another.

Confronting Nietzsche's and Wittgenstein's perspectives shows that the seemingly stark contrast between transformative and descriptive philosophy, between the creative aspects of Nietzsche's philosophy and Wittgenstein's considering of philosophy as 'leaving things as they are', is much weaker than one might initially think. As I hope to have shown, any description involves a creation, and any creation requires a description. In this sense, the task of philosophy for Nietzsche and Wittgenstein aims at a therapeutic redescription of the world and our traditional relation to it. This focus on redescription reveals the poetic dimension of philosophy and how philosophy can bring to see the world anew, and therefore to see oneself anew.

Notes

A tale of two divides

1 'The positivists' answer to this question is equally striking, and it owes more than a passing debt to Nietszche's *Lebensphilosophie* and his critique of metaphysics' (Glock 2008, 118). And 'Mulligan sounds a note of caution. Comparisons between the analytic and continental turns to language are "empty," he maintains, since they disregard the fact that the latter are embedded in various forms of (transcendental) idealism. In my view Nietzsche and Gadamer are clear exceptions to this claim' (Glock 2008, 133).
2 Philosophers have explored various paths to overcome this divide. Lee Braver for instance considers the analytic–continental divide to be analogous to the split between empiricism and rationalism and suggests that dialogue is the only way to overcome the divide. (Braver 2007) The terms 'postanalytic' and 'metacontinental' have been coined as replacements to overcome the divide between analytic and continental (Reynolds et al. 2011).
3 My translation: 'En quoi la poésie demeure un défi pour la pensée du langage. Un défi parce qu'il y a à exposer un conflit que la philosophie rend invisible. Comme elle rend invisible son absence d'une pensée du langage. Parce qu'il y a à mieux comprendre les rapports entre la poésie et la pensée, jusqu'à penser une poétique de la philosophie.'

Chapter 1

1 This shift can be seen through the change of influence of Fritz Mauthner. While Wittgenstein considers to be doing a critique of language 'not in Mauthner's sense' in the *Tractatus* (T. 4.0031), his later work moves in a Mauthnerian direction, as Gershon Weiler argues: 'the change that occurred in Wittgenstein's mind between the *Tractatus* and the *Blue Book* was in a Mauthnerian direction.

I mean, that he came to consider ordinary language as being all right, while discarding the idea of picturing' (Weiler 1958, 86). This Mauthnerian connection is further interesting because, as Janet Lungstrum argues, Mauthner is 'an important bridge between Nietzsche and Wittgenstein' (Lungstrum 1995, 302). Wittgenstein's knowledge of Nietzsche's philosophy thus owes a great deal to Mauthner's works, especially his *Beiträge zu einer Kritik der Sprache*, especially insofar as the influence of Nietzsche on Mauthner is important, as Jacques Le Rider notes: 'We couldn't insist too much on the importance of Nietzsche's text *On Truth and Lie in a Nonmoral Sense* for Fritz Mauthner' (Le Rider 2008). More than Nietzsche, Mauthner is a door to a whole tradition, and according to Michael Forster, Wittgenstein's knowledge of Mauthner's work also explains 'how Wittgenstein became acquainted with the Herder-Hamann tradition's principles' (Forster 2011, 269). As Allan Janik and Stephen Toulmin argue, Mauthner is an influential thinker in 1900 Vienna through which Wittgenstein has come in contact with a general critique of language: 'by the year 1900, the linked problems of communication, authenticity and symbolic expression had been faced in parallel in all the major fields of thought and art. [. . .] So the stage was set for a *philosophical* critique of language, given in completely general terms' (Janik and Toulmin 1996, 119).

2 'On this characterization, therefore, analytical philosophy was born when the "linguistic turn" was taken. This was not, of course, taken uniformly by a group of philosophers at any one time: but the first clear example known to me occurs in Frege's *Die Grundlagen der Arithmetik* of 1884' (Dummett 1993, 5).

3 'The watershed in the development of formal logic, however, was Gottlob Frege's *Begriffsschrift* of 1879' (Glock 2008, 28).

4 It is worth noting that the notions of fiction and metaphor do not exhaust the possibilities of poetic uses of language. However, most philosophers of language reduce poetic and literary uses of language to problems of metaphor and of fiction.

5 This is Derrida's reading of Austin and one of the points of contention in his debate with Searle. Although Searle defends Austin by claiming that rejecting non-serious uses from Ordinary Language Philosophy is a temporary and strategic move, Derrida argues that a strategic move is also a conceptual one and that keeping the distinction between serious and non-serious is keeping the metaphysical distinction between proper and non-proper (Austin 1975, 9–10; 20–2; 104; 121; Derrida 1988; Searle 1977).

6 What is also interesting in the quotation from HH is that the critique of metaphysics through the critique of language is a door to a broader critique of

culture, that is, of all phenomena built on this linguistic fallacy: science, logic, culture in this text, religion, art and morality in many other. This leads to a critique of the value we give to language, especially the exaggeration of the value we give to 'serious things' and the disregard towards 'nearby things' (WS 5 / KSA 2.541).

7   This opposition between metaphors and concepts reflects the broader opposition between expressive and representational conceptions of language: whereas metaphors are lively and unique (because they are part of a process), concepts (and words) attempt to fix and group these metaphors under labels.

8   In a sense, the necessity of generalization is related to Wittgenstein's rejection of the idea of a private language. Without the generalization process of language, we would all be talking about the beetle in our box to use Wittgenstein's image.

9   There are, however, three notable differences between TL and BGE: (1) Nietzsche abandons the term 'metaphor' after 1875. According to Sarah Kofman, there is a shift in vocabulary: 'If Nietzsche substitutes "perspective" for "metaphor," then, it is because the meaning which is posited and transposed in things is no longer referred to an essence of the world, a proper (Kofman 1993, 82). The notion of metaphor retains a metaphysical dimension in the sense that metaphorical meaning is usually thought to be related to and distinct from the literal or proper meaning. The idea that there is such a thing as a proper meaning is a remnant of metaphysics. Moreover, the visual dimension of 'perspective' works well with the idea that metaphor suggests a change in ways of seeing. (2) Nietzsche places the emphasis on the failure of language to account for inner experiences: 'we must also use the same words for the same category of inner experiences; ultimately, we must have the same experience in *common*' (BGE 268 / KAS 5.221). In D 115, he argues that the prejudices embedded in language prevent us from understanding our inner processes and drives because, as Nietzsche argues later in this paragraph from D, our language cannot account for the subtle differences in degrees but only renders the extremes. In other words, language operates a shift from a range of nuances (individual metaphors) to poles (definite concepts). (3) More important than the metaphorical nature of language is the idea that human beings must fix these original metaphors in order to create a common language. This is according to Nietzsche the basis of community, the agreement on the words we use to describe things. But if convention transforms metaphors into words and concepts, a whole system of values is embedded in language. Using Wittgenstein's words, a form of life is embedded in language: '"So you are saying that human agreement decides what is true and what is false?" – It

is what human beings say that is true and false; and they agree in the language they use. That is not agreement in opinions but in form of life' (PI 241). If language is conventional, the notion of agreement is central and at the basis of Wittgenstein's form of life or Nietzsche's community. Through their agreement – and for their agreement to make sense – words and concepts must be stable. Without this stability, if there were only metaphors, we would fall into a form of radical relativism: words could mean anything. John Richardson express as a mismatch between expression and reference: 'On the one hand, language falsifies by equating with one another its referents, what it is about. Here there is a mismatch between words and things and a failure in words' referential use. On the other hand, language also falsifies what we mean to say or express, our thoughts or feelings; once again it does so by an illegitimate equating of (for instance) these feelings with one another. Here there is a mismatch between words and our own attitudes, and a failure in words' expressive use. (Of course, these two uses can run into one another: often one expresses a feeling by naming it.)' (Richardson 2015, 223).

10 The idea of a seduction of language appears in various notes between 1875 and 1884, but also in his published works, BGE and GM especially, see KSA8:6[39]; KSA9:10[D67]; KSA11:26[300]; BGE 16 / KSA 5.29 and GM1 13 / KSA 5.279.

11 Derrida undertakes such a deconstruction of the concept of concept in 'White Mythology' in which he returns to metaphors, following Nietzsche's steps in TL (Derrida 1982, 207–71).

12 Poirier interestingly notes that the separation between ordinary and poetic language is not only the making of philosophers whose theory cannot take poetic uses into account but also of literary scholars who aim to specialize the study of literary language as distinct from the ordinary, as to secure their specificities. These two moves, rejection or sacralization, both make of poetry an exception while a pragmatist philosophy would attempt to make it an ordinary practice (Poirier 1993, 141).

13 This opposition between passive subjects and active agents reflects Deleuze's reading of Nietzsche and his distinction between reactive forces and active forces: 'The power of transformation, the Dionysian power, is the primary definition of activity. But each time we point out the nobility of action and its superiority to reaction in this way we must not forget that reaction also designates a type of force. It is simply that reactions cannot be grasped or scientifically understood as forces if they are not related to superior forces – forces of *another type*. The reactive is a primordial quality of force but one which can only be interpreted as such in relation to and on the basis of the active' (Deleuze 1983, 42). The

power of transformation lies in activity rather than reactivity. Reactive forces a dependent on active forces. Christoph Menke further develops a theory of force that is opposed to capacity: 'Capacity makes us subjects who successfully take part in social practices, insofar as they reproduce their general form. In the play of *forces*, we are pre- and over-subjective agents who are no subjects; active, without self-consciousness; inventive, without aim' (Menke 2013, 13, my translation). While capacity subjects us to a practice, force allows us to become transformative agents.

Chapter 2

1 The classic picture of the history of philosophy considers Herder as Hamann's follower, and indeed, Hamann was Herder's teacher at some point. Regarding matters about language, Forster argues that it was Herder who influenced Hamann rather than the opposite. Whether Herder or Hamann comes first is not my concern here, the important point being that both of them hold similar views on language which have had an impact on later thoughts on language (Forster 2010, 3).
2 Hamann is by the way one of the few philosophers that Wittgenstein mentions in one of his notebooks (Wittgenstein 1997, 40–1).
3 To that extent, a 'magic language' is the antithesis of poetic language which is often characterized as obscure or paradoxical, hence the difficulties for representationalist conceptions of language to account for poetic uses. The focus on use, rather than rejecting poetry as a deviance, can take it into account as a possible use in language. The relation to this use is, however, variable, and we have seen that Heidegger considers it as fundamental whereas Austin considers it a deviance. I will argue in a later chapter that poetic and ordinary language should not be considered as two separate fixed entities for it would re-create, but at another level, a metaphysical conception of language.
4 'In the present century the fragmentary philosophy of Nietzsche's notebooks and of the later Wittgenstein has encouraged the suspicion that Lichtenberg's fragmentary philosophy is of a kind similar to that of Nietzsche or Wittgenstein. For my part I think that anyone who conscientiously seeks "Lichtenberg's philosophy" in the *Sudelbücher* is not exactly wasting his time – no one who reads Lichtenberg conscientiously is wasting his time – but is certainly expending ingenuity in the wrong place: the analogy with Nietzsche or Wittgenstein is misleading, inasmuch as their thinking is only expressed in

fragmentary form whereas Lichtenberg's really is fragmentary' (Lichtenberg 1990, xii–xiii).

5 'Schlegel's use of the fragment is largely the result of his ambivalent relation to creating a system for his ideas. In *Athenäum* Fragment 53 he writes: "It is just as fatal for the spirit to have a system and not to have a system. Some way of combining the two must be reached." According to Eichner, the medium of such a combination is precisely the literary form that the early Romantics favored, the fragment. This form, because it is not *necessarily* systematic, provides the space necessary for the free play of irony and facilitates the possibility that a single idea be approached from a plurality of perspectives' (Millan-Zaibert 2007, 12).

6 Nietzsche considers Hegel's style to be layers of wrapping around an empty kernel: 'For the essence of his style is that a kernel is wrapped round and wrapped round again until it can hardly peep through, bashfully and with inquisitive eyes as "young women peep through their veils," to quote the ancient misogynist Aeschylus – but this kernel is a witty, often indiscreet inspiration on the most intellectual subjects, a daring and subtle phrase-coinage such as is appropriate to the society of thinkers as a condiment to science – but swathed in its wrapping it presents itself as the abstrusest of sciences and altogether a piece of the highest moral boredom!' (D 193 / KSA 3.166-7) Nietzsche's critique of Spinoza as a systematic writer with his 'hocus-pocus of mathematical form' (BGE 5 / KSA 5.19) also goes in this direction; he is against a philosophy which would not include poetry.

7 My translation: 'la réflexion sur la textualité philosophique devient un problème philosophique avec [Schlegel].'

8 'For the historian and the poet differ not by speaking in metrical verse or without meter (for it would be possible to put the writings of Herodotus into meter, and they would be a history with meter no less than without it)' (Aristotle 2006, 32, 1451b).

9 Richard Eldridge further argues that Wittgenstein's philosophy shares important characteristics with Romanticism: 'So much can be gleaned from a Wittgensteinian vision of language and mind in conjunction with a Cavellian reading of it. Is it convincing? There can be, again, no neutral, demonstrative argument in favor of it, independent of the focusing or transfiguring of a perception of our condition. But it may help to elaborate the depth and imaginative appeal of this vision of our immigrant condition to see how much it shares with Hölderlin's philosophical Romanticism and its consequences in Hölderlin's poetic practice' (Eldridge 2001, 238). This Romantic connection is interesting also because it places aesthetics at a prominent position, as

Clinton Verdonschot shows that 'reading Wittgenstein under an early German Romanticist light will allow us to make sense of the idea of aesthetic reasons. Aesthetic reasons ground the way in which we make sense of the world, while remaining groundless themselves' (Verdonschot 2021, 81).

10 In his later works, Heidegger uses the word 'thinking' rather than 'philosophy'. For Heidegger, 'philosophy' is metaphysics. Once metaphysics has been brought to its end (because of Nietzsche's inversion of Platonism), the word 'philosophy' needs replacing. Heidegger uses 'thinking': 'A thinking which can be neither metaphysics nor science' (Heidegger 1977, 378).

11 Let us note that Heidegger's notion of logic has little, if not nothing, to do with that of the logical positivists' such as Carnap whose criticism of Heidegger is one of the important steps in the history of the analytic–continental divide. However, this opposition marks rather a confrontation between two philosophers than the radical rejection of one philosophical tradition by another. Andrea Vrahimis argues that the reason for the divide is to be found in 'extra-philosophical factors' rather than philosophical ones: 'In all of these encounters, it is not some irreconcilable clash between philosophical movements which is to be found; rather, extra-philosophical factors cause such misinterpretations. [. . .] This series of mistakes and omissions are caused by a drive towards picturing twentieth century philosophy as split in two, and have been instrumental in painting the haunting image of such a split. Philosophers have committed these mistakes because they were seeking some justification for this image of itself that philosophy had conjured. In the attempts to shout across the gulf, one might have expected to find an explanation for the prevailing silence. But perhaps such efforts precluded looking closely enough in order to see the flawed nature of the object of their enquiry. Thus, it is not without at least some small element of surprise or disbelief that one may discover proximity between thinkers who had been imagined to lie so far apart' (Vrahimis 2013, 182).

Chapter 3

1 I focus here only on expressivism in philosophy of language. It is important to note that this notion is usually more widely used and discussed in metaethics.

2 The extent to which all statements are expressive rather than representative is an ongoing debate opposing 'local expressivists' like Simon Blackburn to 'global expressivists' like Huw Price. However, Matthew Simpson argues that none of the expressivists projects actually count as global and that 'the debate

between the localists and the globalists is merely verbal, about what theories count as expressivist' (Simpson 2020, 159). My argument is not related to this debate insofar as I argue only that a certain form of expressivism is necessary to account for poetic phenomena. It is interesting, however, to note that Romantic expressivism would be considered a rather radical form of expressivism, one that few contemporary philosophers would actually follow.

3   This rooting in a history of philosophy is especially visible in his *Tales of the Mighty Dead* in which he traces the history of inferentialism back to Spinoza and Leibniz. His most recent book, *A Spirit of Trust*, presents itself as a reading of Hegel and reveals how his philosophy inherits from the Hegelian project (Brandom 2002; 2019).

4   In that sense, Brandom follows Austin in considering poetic language as a ditch surrounding ordinary language, as Derrida suggests in his reading of Austin (Derrida 1988, 17). Maximilian de Gaynesford considers this opposition as one between analytic philosophers and literary critics: 'When analytic philosophers deny that poetry is or could be serious, they overlook what is genuinely troubling about this attitude. And equally, when poets and literary critics respond to this attitude, they exaggerate what is disturbing about it, treating as professional aversion what is no worse than odious group levity, and so reinforce a parallel disinclination to treat philosophy seriously' (de Gaynesford 2017, 13).

5   Derrida notes an insightful connection between Austin and Nietzsche around the notion of force, showing the shift from truth-value to value of force that is also at work in pragmatism and expressivism: 'Austin was obliged to free the analysis of the performative from the authority of the truth *value*, from the true/false opposition at least in its classical form, and to substitute for it at times the value of force, of difference of force (*illocutionary* or *perlocutionary force*). (In this line of thought, which is nothing less than Nietzschean, this in particular strikes me as moving in the direction of Nietzsche himself, who often acknowledged a certain affinity for a vein of English thought.)' (Derrida 1988, 13). This replacement of truth-value by force opens a new field of possibilities for thinking language (Lorenzini 2017). I have argued that it is especially insightful to approach poetic uses of language (Mills 2021).

6   This idea echoes in some ways Donald Davidson's characterization of metaphors. Davidson argues that there is no metaphorical meaning, but that metaphors present statements that are either patently false or trivially true which brings us to see things differently. To a broader extent, what poetic uses of language might show us is a specific attention to language which brings us to see and use language differently (Davidson 2001).

7   The relation between Nietzsche and naturalism is a rather complex and contested one, and my aim here is not to settle this question. My claim will be to consider Nietzsche as an expressivist (whether this entails a naturalism is another matter). But if there is a naturalism in Nietzsche, it is certainly not a scientific one and could hence be related to Price's subject naturalism.

Chapter 4

1. As Tiger Roholt argues regarding philosophy of music (but the same could be said of philosophy of poetry, and of all artforms), there is mainly a methodological distinction: 'that it is a *methodological tendency* of continental philosophers of music to resist methodological detachment in two basic ways. And it is a methodological tendency of analytic philosophers of music to detach *in one or both* of these ways' (Roholt 2017). For Roholt, analytic philosophy of music attempts to separate the study of music from the context whereas continental philosophy emphasizes context. Although this distinction is, as all distinctions between analytic and continental philosophy, somewhat schematic, it highlights a difference in the aims and scope of philosophical study of an art form.
2. Following a similar line of thought, Werner Stegmaier considers that Nietzsche offers no doctrine but only signs which point us in one direction (Stegmaier 2006). Without going as far, we can say that Nietzsche's positive views (what could be called elements of a doctrine) must never be taken absolutely but only perspectivally.
3. 'Be this as it may, Wittgenstein was not a poet but a philosopher. And philosophy enters with Wittgenstein the stage which has been reached by many another creative activity of the human mind – by poetry, for instance, or by painting: the stage where every act of creation is inseparable from the critique of its medium, and every work, intensely reflecting upon itself, looks like the embodied doubt of its own possibility. It is a predicament which Nietzsche uncannily anticipated in a sketch entitled "A Fragment from the History of Posterity"' (Heller 1988, 157).
4. Recent accounts of Nietzsche's expressivism consider it from the perspective of action rather than language. According to Aaron Ridley, 'Expressivism, then, is the view that the content of our will becomes fully determinate only in the states of affairs in which it is realized' (Ridley 2018, 6). Similarly, Robert Pippin considers: '"Expressivism" is a claim that shares an assumption with all accounts of action as such – that there are bodily movements or mental happenings that stand in a relation to a subject's mindedness – and it argues for a kind of relation different

from all causal, compatibilist and voluntarist, free-will accounts' (Pippin 2015, 233). Both these accounts, although they focus on action and not on language, consider that the relation between will and action is not to be thought in the traditional causal sense, but in an expressive sense, thus mirroring the idea that language is not to be thought in terms of reference, but that the relation between word and world is of a different nature.

5 A metaphorical statement might indeed be factually false, and Donald Davidson argues that metaphorical statements need to be either patently false or trivially true (Davidson 2001, 259).

6 My translation: 'L'art et la poésie ont bien trait à la vérité, mais cette vérité n'est pas de même nature que celle à laquelle aspire la science. [. . .] La science énonce des propositions dont on découvre qu'elles sont vraies ou fausses en les confrontant aux faits qu'elles cherchent à décrire. [. . .] Il s'agit là d'une vérité de correspondance ou d'adéquation. Lorsqu'en revanche Baudelaire dit que "le Poète est semblable au prince des nuées", c'est-à-dire à l'albatros, il est impossible de procéder à une vérification, et pourtant Baudelaire ne dit pas n'importe quoi, il cherche à nous révéler l'identité du poète; cette fois-ci, il aspire à une vérité de dévoilement, il tente de mettre en évidence la nature d'un être, d'une situation, d'un monde. A chaque fois, un rapport s'établit entre mots et monde, pourtant les deux vérités ne se confondent pas. [. . .] On peut conclure que non seulement l'art conduit à la connaissance du monde, mais il révèle en même temps l'existence de cette vérité dont la nature est différente. En réalité, celle-ci ne lui appartient pas exclusivement, puisqu'elle constitue l'horizon des autres discours interprétatifs: histoire, sciences humaines, philosophie.'

Chapter 5

1 The whole DD can be read as following this anti-Platonic line of thought, and that there is a continuity in the poems that mirror Zarathustra's journey (Mills 2020).

2 This thesis has been famously defended by Roman Jakobson who considers that the poetic function of language precisely lies in the self-referentiality of the message: 'The set toward the message as such, focus on the message for its own sake, is the poetic function of language' (Jakobson 1960, 356). While this view has been influential throughout the twentieth century, the poetic function of language does not describe all that is done in poetry and can also be found to various degrees in many uses of language.

3 My translation: '[Poésie et langage courant] se réalisent dans une inséparation du son et du sens. Parce que l'empirique du langage est en grande partie manqué par le modèle du signe. Banalement, et dans toutes les activités du langage, c'est le discours qui est premier et non l'unité mot, qui est le lieu de la séparation entre le son est le sens. Et du poème ne commence que quand le continu d'une sémantique sérielle travaille un discours. Dans une inséparation de l'affect et du concept.'

4 As Joachim Schulte argues, the difference between information and poetry does not occur on the grounds of meaning but on those of use: 'The terms "information" and "communication" are far too comprehensive and too vague to permit any drawing of boundaries around uses for the purpose of information or communication. I think that Wittgenstein merely wants to say that poetry, even though it employs the same building blocks as ordinary ("prosaic") speech, is subject to different conventions from those regulating the manifold kinds of uses of language which serve to impart information and to communicate facts. And of course Wittgenstein does not want to deny that poetry can be used to communicate all sorts of information. He only reminds us of the fact that if poetry is used *as poetry* it is not (mainly) used to give information; and that if it is chiefly used to convey information it is not really used *as poetry* – it may, for instance, be employed in an, as it were, "quotational" way' (Gibson and Huemer 2004, 154–5).

5 An important distinction to make here, however, is that both seeing a duck and seeing a rabbit are meaningful, are seeing something, whereas reading a poem as a meaningless series of words is not meaningful and is like reading nothing. However, we could argue that reading a poem as a meaningless series of words is like searching (and failing to find) for the rabbit while seeing the duck. A failure to understand a poem, therefore a failure to read it as something else than a meaningless series of words, is like failing to see the rabbit while looking for it.

6 Conceptual poetry like the 'uncreative writing' practised by Kenneth Goldsmith among others seems to push this idea even further by bringing attention to the very ordinary language of weather, traffic or sports reports (Goldsmith 2005; 2007; 2008).

7 This idea of decontextualization can also be found in the works of the Russian Formalists, especially Viktor Shklovsky who discusses this extensively in his article 'Art as Device'. Following Tolstoy, he elaborates the notion of 'ostranenie': 'The goal of art is to create the sensation of seeing, and not merely recognizing, things; the device of art is the "*ostranenie*" of things and complication of the form, which increases the duration and complexity of perception, as the process of perception is its own end in art and must be prolonged' (Shklovsky 2017, 80). Through the 'ostranenie' or defamiliarization, art brings viewers and reader to see

things differently. However, Shklovsky's theory still attempts to define poetry in essentialist terms by defining poetic language as different from ordinary language: 'Thus, we arrive at a definition of poetry as decelerated, contorted speech' (Shklovsky 2017, 95).

Chapter 6

1. Alison Denham interestingly argues that poetry does not only make us 'see as' but 'experience as', thus including not only perceptual experience through the senses but also affective responses: 'So described, experiencing-as, like perceptual experience more generally, is not confined to the five senses, even if it occurs by way of them: affective responses such as emotions, moods, and motivational dispositions are also embodied, first-personal, and phenomenologically characterize' (Gibson 2015, 184). The idea of experiencing-as allows to consider the epistemic value of poetry regarding ethical questions for instance.
2. Alexander Nehamas is the most famous Nietzsche scholar to connect perspectivism to aesthetics as he considers Nietzsche's perspectivism to be connected to aestheticism in two ways: first, aestheticism is part of the motivation for perspectivism as Nietzsche 'looks at the world in general as if it were a sort of artwork; in particular, he looks at it as if it were a literary text' (Nehamas 1985, 3). Second, this philology of the world 'not only provides him with a literary model for many of his views but also motivates him to create what we may well call a literary product' (Nehamas 1985, 4). These two ideas reflect how what I call a perspectival poetics brings to a poetic world view and a poetics of philosophy.
3. Perspectivism has indeed become an important strand in contemporary epistemology but has done so by extracting itself from the Nietzschean realm. For instance, Michaela Massimi advocates for perspectivism as a 'middle ground between scientific realism and antirealism' by referring not to Nietzsche (whom she nevertheless mentions en passant) but to Kant, a much more common figure in epistemological research (Saatsi 2018, 164–75).
4. The only time Hales and Welshon discuss the notion of perception in Nietzsche is in relation to Leibniz's distinction between 'perception', 'sensation' and 'apperception'. They, however, do not attempt to relate their discussion of perception to perspectivism, although there is a connection between perspectivism and Leibniz (Hales and Welshon 2000, 136–7).
5. In Sophie Fiennes's documentary *The Pervert's Guide to Cinema*, Žižek analyses John Carpenter's film *They Live* and suggests a similar violence to change

ideology. In this film, the main character finds glasses which show him the message behind advertising, and a fight ensues his attempt to bring from his friend to use the glasses. Ideology is so embedded in us that, Žižek argues, violence is sometimes necessary to question it (Fiennes 2006).

6. The child-poet can be related to Nietzsche's philosopher of the future who must have a perspectival education (Mills 2019b).

Conclusion

1. 'If you read German books you find not the faintest memory of the need for a technique, a teaching plan, a will to mastery in thinking – of the fact that thinking needs to be learned just as dancing needs to be learned, as a kind of dancing. [. . .] For you cannot subtract every form of dancing from a noble education, the ability to dance with the feet, with concepts, with words; do I still need to say that you must also be able to dance with the pen – that you must learn to write?' (TI 'Germans' 7 / KSA 6.109-10).

2. Although I have not focused on this aspect in the course of my argument, it is worth noting that the understanding of philosophy as a therapy is a point where Nietzsche and Wittgenstein converge. (Mills 2019a)

3. 'In other words, the touchstone of philosophy in the Continental tradition might be said to be *practice;* that is to say, our historically and culturally embedded life in the world as finite selves. It is this touchstone of practice that leads philosophy towards a critique of present conditions, as conditions not amenable to freedom, and to the Utopian demand that things be otherwise, the demand for a transformative practice of philosophy, art, poetry or thinking' (Critchley 1997, 357).

Bibliography

Abrams, Meyer Howard. 1977. *The Mirror and the Lamp: Romantic Theory and the Critical Tradition*. Oxford: Oxford University Press.

Altieri, Charles. 2015. *Reckoning with the Imagination: Wittgenstein and the Aesthetics of Literary Experience*. Ithaca and London: Cornell University Press.

Apel, Karl-Otto. 1967. 'Wittgenstein Und Heidegger. Die Frage Nach Dem Sinn von Sein Und Der Sinnlosigkeitsverdacht Gegen Alle Metaphysik'. *Philosophisches Jahrbuch* 75: 56–94.

Aristotle. 2006. *Poetics*. Translated by Joe Sachs. Newburyport, MA: Focus Publishing.

Austin, J. L. 1975. *How to Do Things with Words*. Edited by J. O. Urmson and Marina Sbisà. Cambridge, MA: Harvard University Press.

Ayer, Alfred Jules, ed. 1959. *Logical Positivism*. Glencoe, IL: The Free Press.

Ayer, Alfred Jules. 1971. *Russell and Moore: The Analytical Heritage*. London and Basingstoke: MacMillan.

Babich, Babette E. 1994. *Nietzsche's Philosophy of Science: Reflecting on the Ground of Art and Life*. Albany, NY: SUNY Press.

Baghramian, Maria. 2004. *Relativism*. London and New York: Routledge.

Bernstein, J. M. 2003. *Classic and Romantic: German Aesthetics*. Cambridge: Cambridge University Press.

Biletzki, Anat, and Anat Matar, eds. 2012. *The Story of Analytic Philosophy: Plot and Heroes*. London and New York: Routledge.

Blackburn, Simon. 2007. *Truth: A Guide*. Oxford: Oxford University Press.

Bowie, Andrew. 1997. *From Romanticism to Critical Theory the Philosophy of German Literary Theory*. London and New York: Routledge.

Bowie, Andrew. 2000. 'The Romantic Connection: Neurath, the Frankfurt School, and Heidegger. Part One'. *British Journal for the History of Philosophy* 8 (2): 275–98.

Brandom, Robert B. 2002. *Tales of the Mighty Dead: Historical Essays in the Metaphysics of Intentionality*. Cambridge, MA and London: Harvard University Press.

Brandom, Robert B. 2003. *Articulating Reasons: An Introduction to Inferentialism*. Cambridge, MA and London: Harvard University Press.

Brandom, Robert B. 2008. *Between Saying and Doing: Towards an Analytic Pragmatism*. Oxford: Oxford University Press.

Brandom, Robert B. 2011. *Perspectives on Pragmatism: Classical, Recent, and Contemporary*. Cambridge, MA and London: Harvard University Press.

Brandom, Robert B. 2019. *A Spirit of Trust: A Reading of Hegel's Phenomenology*. Cambridge, MA and London: Harvard University Press.

Braver, Lee. 2007. *A Thing of This World: A History of Continental Anti-Realism*. Evanston, IL: Northwestern University Press.

Braver, Lee. 2012. *Groundless Grounds: A Study of Wittgenstein and Heidegger*. Cambridge, MA: MIT Press.

Brobjer, Thomas H. 2008. *Nietzsche's Philosophical Context: An Intellectual Biography*. Urbana: University of Illinois Press.

Campbell, John. 2012. 'Cogito Ergo Sum: Christopher Peacocke and John Campbell: II—Lichtenberg and the Cogito'. *Proceedings of the Aristotelian Society* 112: 361–78.

Cavell, Stanley. 1964. 'Existentialism and Analytical Philosophy'. *Daedalus Daedalus* 93 (3): 946–74.

Cavell, Stanley. 1976. *Must We Mean What We Say?* Cambridge: Cambridge University Press.

Cavell, Stanley. 1979. *The Claim of Reason Wittgenstein, Skepticism, Morality, and Tragedy*. Oxford: Clarendon Press.

Clark, Maudemarie. 1990. *Nietzsche on Truth and Philosophy*. Cambridge: Cambridge University Press.

Cloeren, Hermann J. 1988. *Language and Thought: German Approaches to Analytic Philosophy in the 18th and 19th Centuries*. Berlin and New York: De Gruyter.

Conant, James. 2005. 'The Dialectic of Perspectivism, I'. *Sats : Nordic Journal of Philosophy* 6 (2): 5–50.

Cook, Jon, ed. 2004. *Poetry in Theory an Anthology 1900-2000*. Malden, MA: Blackwell.

Cox, Christoph. 1997. 'The "Subject" of Nietzsche's Perspectivism'. *Journal of the History of Philosophy* 35 (2): 269.

Critchley, Simon. 1997. 'What Is Continental Philosophy?'. *International Journal of Philosophical Studies* 5 (3): 347–63.

Danto, Arthur. 2005. *Nietzsche as Philosopher*. New York: Columbia University Press.

Davidson, Donald. 2001. *Inquiries into Truth and Interpretation*. Oxford: Clarendon Press.

Deleuze, Gilles. 1983. *Nietzsche and Philosophy*. Translated by Hugh Tomlinson. New York: Columbia University Press.

Deleuze, Gilles, and Claire Parnet. 1996. *L'Abécédaire de Gilles Deleuze 1988-1989*. Sodaperaga Productions and La Fémis.

Derrida, Jacques. 1982. *Margins of Philosophy*. Translated by Alan Bass. Chicago and London: University of Chicago Press.

Derrida, Jacques. 1988. *Limited Inc*. Edited by Gerald Graff. Translated by Jeffrey Mehlman and Samuel Weber. Evanston, IL: Northwestern University Press.

Descartes, René. 2006. *A Discourse on the Method of Correctly Conducting One's Reason and Seeking Truth in the Sciences*. Translated by Ian Maclean. Oxford: Oxford University Press.

Dummett, Michael. 1978. *Truth and Other Enigmas*. London: Duckworth.

Dummett, Michael. 1993. *Origins of Analytical Philosophy*. Cambridge, MA and London: Harvard University Press.

Eldridge, Richard Thomas. 2001. *The Persistence of Romanticism: Essays in Philosophy and Literature*. Cambridge: Cambridge University Press.

Fiennes, Sophie. 2006. *The Pervert's Guide to Cinema*. London: P. Guide.

Fish, Stanley. 1982. *Is There a Text in This Class?* Cambridge, MA and London: Harvard University Press.

Forster, Michael. 2010. *After Herder: Philosophy of Language in the German Tradition*. Oxford: Oxford University Press.

Forster, Michael. 2011. *German Philosophy of Language From Schlegel to Hegel and Beyond*. Oxford: Oxford University Press.

Frank, Manfred. 1999. 'Style in Philosophy: Parts II and III'. *Metaphilosophy* 30 (4): 264–301.

Frege, Gottlob. 1997. *The Frege Reader*. Edited by Michael Beaney. Malden, MA: Blackwell.

Gaynesford, Maximilian de. 2017. *The Rift in the Lute: Attuning Poetry and Philosophy*. Oxford: Oxford University Press.

Gibson, John, ed. 2015. *The Philosophy of Poetry*. Oxford: Oxford University Press.

Gibson, John, and Wolfgang Huemer, eds. 2004. *The Literary Wittgenstein*. London: Routledge.

Glock, Hans-Johann. 2008. *What Is Analytic Philosophy?* Cambridge: Cambridge University Press.

Goldsmith, Kenneth. 2005. *The Weather*. Los Angeles: Make Now.

Goldsmith, Kenneth. 2007. *Traffic*. Los Angeles: Make Now.

Goldsmith, Kenneth. 2008. *Sports*. Los Angeles: Make Now.

Goodman, Nelson. 1995. *Ways of Worldmaking*. Indianapolis: Hackett.

Gori, Pietro. 2019. *Nietzsche's Pragmatism: A Study on Perspectival Thought*. Translated by Sarah De Sanctis. Berlin and Boston: De Gruyter.

Hacker, Peter. 2015. 'Forms of Life'. *Nordic Wittgenstein Review* Special Issue: Wittgenstein and Forms of Life: 1–20.

Hales, Steven D., and Rex Welshon. 2000. *Nietzsche's Perspectivism*. Urbana: University of Illinois Press.

Hamann, Johann Georg. 2007. *Writings on Philosophy and Language*. Translated by Kenneth Haynes. Cambridge: Cambridge University Press.

Hanna, Patricia, and Bernard Harrison. 2004. *Word and World: Practice and the Foundations of Language*. Cambridge: Cambridge University Press.

Heidegger, Martin. 1977. *Basic Writings: From Being and Time (1927) to The Task of Thinking (1964)*. Translated by David Farrell Krell. New York: Harper Collins.

Heidegger, Martin. 1982. *On the Way to Language*. Translated by Peter Donald Hertz. New York: Harper Collins.

Heidegger, Martin. 2004. *On the Essence of Language: The Metaphysics of Language and the Essencing of the Word; Concerning Herder's Treatise On the Origin of Language*. Translated by Wanda Torres Gregory and Yvonne Unna. Albany, NY: SUNY Press.

Heidegger, Martin. 2009. *Logic as the Question Concerning the Essence of Language*. Translated by Wanda Torres Gregory and Yvonne Unna. Albany, NY: SUNY Press.

Heidegger, Martin. 2011. *Introduction to Philosophy - Thinking and Poetizing*. Translated by Phillip Jacques Braunstein. Bloomington: Indiana University Press.

Heidegger, Martin. 2013. *Poetry, Language, Thought*. Translated by Albert Hofstadter. New York: Harper & Row.

Heller, Erich. 1988. *The Importance of Nietzsche: Ten Essays*. Chicago and London: The University of Chicago Press.

Herder, Johann Gottfried von. 2002. *Herder: Philosophical Writings*. Edited by Michael Forster. Cambridge: Cambridge University Press.

Higgins, Kathleen Marie. 2000. *Comic Relief: Nietzsche's Gay Science*. Oxford: Oxford University Press.

Humboldt, Wilhelm von. 1999. *On Language: On the Diversity of Human Language Construction and Its Influence on the Mental Development of the Human Species*. Translated by Peter Heath and Michael Losonsky. Cambridge: Cambridge University Press.

Jakobson, Roman. 1960. 'Closing Statement: Linguistics and Poetics'. In *Style in Language*, edited by Thomas A. Sebeck, 350–77. Cambridge, MA: MIT Press.

Janik, Allan, and Stephen Edelston Toulmin. 1996. *Wittgenstein's Vienna*. Chicago: Elephant Paperbakcs.

Kivy, Peter, ed. 2004. *The Blackwell Guide to Aesthetics*. Malden, MA: Blackwell.

Kofman, Sarah. 1993. *Nietzsche and Metaphor*. Translated by Duncan Large. Stanford: Stanford University Press.

Kristeva, Julia. 1984. *Revolution in Poetic Language*. Translated by Margaret Waller. New York: Columbia University Press.

Le Rider, Jacques. 2008. 'Crise du Langage et Position Mystique: le Moment 1901–1903, autour de Fritz Mauthner'. *Germanica* 43: 13–27.

Lichtenberg, Georg Christoph. 1990. *The Waste Books*. Translated by R. J Hollingdale. New York: New York Review Books.

Lichtenberg, Georg Christoph. 2012. *Philosophical Writings*. Translated by Steven Tester. Albany, NY: SUNY Press.

Lightbody. 2020. 'Hermeneutics vs. Genealogy: Brandom's Cloak or Nietzsche's Quilt?'. *The European Legacy* 25 (6): 635–52.

Lorenzini, Daniele. 2017. *La Force du vrai: de Foucault à Austin*. Lormont: Le bord de l'eau.

Lungstrum, Janet. 1995. 'Wittgenstein and Nietzsche Agonal Relations in Language'. *Deutsche Vierteljahrsschrift Für Literaturwissenschaft Und Geistesgeschichte* 69 (2): 300–23.

Lycan, William G. 2008. *Philosophy of Language: A Contemporary Introduction*. London and New York: Routledge.

Majetschak, Stefan. 2007. *Ästhetik zur Einführung*. Hamburg: Junius.

Martin, Glen T. 1989. *From Nietzsche to Wittgenstein: The Problem of Truth and Nihilism in the Modern World*. New York: Peter Lang.

Menke, Christoph. 2013. *Die Kraft der Kunst*. Berlin: Suhrkamp.

Meschonnic, Henri. 2001. *Célébration de la poésie*. Lagrasse: Verdier.

Millan-Zaibert, Elizabeth. 2007. *Friedrich Schlegel and the Emergence of Romantic Philosophy*. Ithaca: SUNY Press.

Mills, Philip. 2019a. 'La Philosophie Comme Thérapie Chez Nietzsche et Wittgenstein'. In *Die Frage Der Medizin in Nietzsches Philosophie / La Question de La Médecine Dans La Philosophie de Nietzsche*, edited by Isabelle Wienand and Patrick Wotling, 347–66. Basel and Berlin: Schwabe Verlag.

Mills, Philip. 2019b. 'L'enfant de Zarathoustra : Figure Poétique de l'affirmation Créatrice'. In *Nietzsche, Penseur de l'affirmation. Relecture d'Ainsi Parlait Zarathoustra*, edited by Clément Bertot, Jean Leclerq, Nicolas Monseu, and Patrick Wotling, 209–16. Louvain-la-Neuve: Presses Universitaires de Louvain.

Mills, Philip. 2020. '"Rien qu'un fou ! Rien qu'un poète !" : Lecture des Dithyrambes de Dionysos comme inversion du platonisme'. In *Nietzsche: les textes de 1888*, edited by Céline Denat and Patrick Wotling, 159–67. Reims: Epure.

Mills, Philip. 2021. 'Doing Things with Words The Transformative Force of Poetry'. *Croatian Journal of Philosophy* 21 (61): 111–33.

Monk, Ray. 1991. *Ludwig Wittgenstein: The Duty of Genius*. New York: Penguin Books.

Nehamas, Alexander. 1985. *Nietzsche, Life as Literature*. Cambridge, MA and London: Harvard University Press.

Nietzsche, Friedrich. 1974. *The Gay Science*. Translated by Walter Kaufmann. New York: Vintage Books.

Nietzsche, Friedrich. 1995. *Human, All Too Human I*. Translated by Gary Handwerk. Stanford: Stanford University Press.

Nietzsche, Friedrich. 2001. *Dithyrambs of Dionysus (Dionysos-Dithyramben)*. Translated by R. J Hollingdale. London: Anvil Press.

Nietzsche, Friedrich. 2008a. *Beyond Good and Evil: Prelude to a Philosophy of the Future*. Translated by Marion Faber. Oxford: Oxford University Press.

Nietzsche, Friedrich. 2008b. *On the Genealogy of Morals*. Translated by Douglas Smith. Oxford: Oxford University Press.

Nietzsche, Friedrich. 2008c. *The Birth of Tragedy*. Translated by Douglas Smith. Oxford and New York: Oxford University Press.

Nietzsche, Friedrich. 2008d. *Thus Spoke Zarathustra: A Book for Everyone and No One*. Translated by Graham Parkes. Oxford: Oxford University Press.

Nietzsche, Friedrich. 2008e. *Twilight of the Idols*. Translated by Duncan Large. Oxford: Oxford University Press.

Nietzsche, Friedrich. 2009a. *Sämtliche Werke: Kritische Studienausgabe in 15 Bänden*. Edited by Giorgio Colli and Mazzino Montinari. Berlin and New York: de Gruyter.

Nietzsche, Friedrich. 2009b. *Writings from the Early Notebooks*. Edited by Raymond Geuss and Alexander Nehamas. Translated by Ladislaus Löb. Cambridge and New York: Cambridge University Press.

Nietzsche, Friedrich. 2010. *The Peacock and the Buffalo: The Poetry of Nietzsche*. Translated by James Luchte. London and New York: Continuum.

Nietzsche, Friedrich. 2012. *Human, All Too Human II and Unpublished Fragments from the Period of 'Human, All Too Human II' (Spring 1878–Fall 1879)*. Translated by Gary Handwerk. Stanford: Stanford University Press.

Nietzsche, Friedrich. 2015. *Daybreak: Thoughts on the Prejudices of Morality*. Edited by Maudemarie Clark and Brian Leiter. Translated by R.J Hollingdale. Cambridge: Cambridge University Press.

Novalis. 1997. *Philosophical Writings*. Translated by Margaret Mahony Stoljar. Albany, NY: SUNY Press.

O'Grady, Paul. 2004. 'Wittgenstein and Relativism'. *International Journal of Philosophical Studies* 12 (3): 315–37.

Perloff, Marjorie. 1996. *Wittgenstein's Ladder: Poetic Language and the Strangeness of the Ordinary*. Chicago and London: University of Chicago Press.

Pippin, Robert B., ed. 2015. *Interanimations: Receiving Modern German Philosophy*. Chicago and London: University of Chicago Press.

Plato. 1997. *Complete Works*. Edited by John M. Cooper and D. S. Hutchinson. Indianapolis and Cambridge: Hackett.

Poirier, Richard. 1993. *Poetry and Pragmatism*. Cambridge, MA and London: Harvard University Press.

Ponge, Francis. 1974. *The Voice of Things*. Translated by Beth Archer. New York: McGraw-Hill Book Co.

Pouivet, Roger. 2000. 'Esthétique anglo-américaine et métaphysique'. *Revue française d'études américaines* 86: 37–48.

Price, Huw. 2011. *Naturalism without Mirrors*. Oxford: Oxford University Press.

Price, Huw. 2013. *Expressivism, Pragmatism and Representationalism*. Cambridge: Cambridge University Press.

Price, Huw. 2019. 'Global Expressivism by the Method of Differences'. Edited by Mariá J. Frápolli. *Royal Institute of Philosophy Supplement* 86: 133–54.

Rancière, Jacques. 2011. *Mute Speech: Literature, Critical Theory, and Politics*. Translated by James Swenson. New York: Columbia University Press.

Reynolds, Jack, James Chase, James A. Williams, and Ed Mares, eds. 2011. *Postanalytic and Metacontinental: Crossing Philosophical Divides*. London and New York: Bloomsbury.

Richardson, John. 2015. 'Nietzsche, Language, Community'. In *Individual and Community in Nietzsche's Philosophy*, edited by Julian Young, 214–43. Cambridge: Cambridge University Press.

Ricoeur, Paul. 2007. *The Conflict of Interpretations*. Translated by Don Ihde. Evanston, IL: Northwestern University Press.

Ridley, Aaron. 2018. *The Deed Is Everything: Nietzsche on Will and Action*. Oxford: Oxford University Press.

Roholt, Tiger. 2017. 'On the Divide: Analytic and Continental Philosophy of Music'. *JAAC The Journal of Aesthetics and Art Criticism* 75 (1): 49–58.

Rorty, Richard. 1981. 'Nineteenth-Century Idealism and Twentieth-Century Textualism'. *The Monist* 64 (2): 155–74.

Rorty, Richard. 1989. *Contingency, Irony, and Solidarity*. Cambridge: Cambridge University Press.

Rorty, Richard. 2009. *Philosophy and the Mirror of Nature*. Princeton: Princeton University Press.

Rorty, Richard. 2016. *Philosophy as Poetry*. Charlottesville and London: University of Virginia Press.

Saatsi, Juha, ed. 2018. *The Routledge Handbook of Scientific Realism*. London and New York: Routledge.

Saussure, Ferdinand de. 2011. *Course in General Linguistics*. Edited by Perry Meisel and Haun Saussy. Translated by Wade Baskin. New York: Columbia University Press.

Schacht, Richard. 1974. 'Philosophy as Linguistic Analysis: A Nietzschean Critique'. *Philosophical Studies* 25 (3): 153–71.

Schlegel, Friedrich. 1855. *The Philosophy of Life, and Philosophy of Language: In a Course of Lectures*. Translated by A. J. W Morrison. New York: Harper.

Schrift, Alan D. 1990. *Nietzsche and the Question of Interpretation: Between Hermeneutics and Deconstruction*. London and New York: Routledge.

Searle, John R. 1977. 'Reiterating the Differences: A Reply to Jacques Derrida'. *Glyph*, 198–208.

Shklovsky, Viktor. 2017. *Viktor Shklovsky. A Reader*. Translated by Alexandra Berlina. London and New York: Bloomsbury.

Simpson, Matthew. 2020. 'What Is Global Expressivism?'. *The Philosophical Quarterly* 70 (278): 140–61.

Stegmaier, Werner. 2006. 'Nietzsche's Doctrines, Nietzsche's Signs'. *Journal of Nietzsche Studies* 31 (1): 20–41.

Stingelin, Martin. 1996. *'Unsere Ganze Philosophie ist Berichtigung des Sprachgebrauchs': Friedrich Nietzsches Lichtenberg-Rezeption im Spannungsfeld zwischen Sprachkritik (Rhetorik) und historischer kritik (Genealogie)*. München: Wilhelm Fink Verlag.

Strong, Tracy B. 1985. 'Text and Pretexts: Reflections on Perspectivism in Nietzsche'. *Politicaltheory Political Theory* 13 (2): 164–82.

Taylor, Charles. 1985. *Philosophical Papers: Volume 1, Human Agency and Language*. Cambridge and New York: Cambridge University Press.

Taylor, Charles. 2016. *The Language Animal: The Full Shape of the Human Linguistic Capacity*. Cambridge, MA and London: Belknap Press of Harvard University Press.

Tempest, Kate. 2014. *Everybody Down*. Big Dada, London.

Thouard, Denis. 2001. 'La question de la « forme de la philosophie » dans le romantisme allemand'. *Methodos* 1. http://journals.openedition.org/methodos/47.

Todorov, Tzvetan. 2007. *La littérature en péril*. Paris: Flammarion.

Underhill, James W. 2009. *Humboldt, Worldview and Language*. Edinburgh: Edinburgh University Press.

Verdonschot, Clinton Peter. 2021. '"That They Point Is All There Is to It": Wittgenstein's Romanticist Aesthetics'. *Estetika: The European Journal of Aesthetics* 58 (1): 72–88.

Vrahimis, Andreas. 2013. *Encounters Between Analytic and Continental Philosophy Across the Abyss*. Basingstoke: Palgrave Macmillan.

Weiler, Gershon. 1958. 'On Fritz Mauthner's Critique of Language'. *Mind* 67 (265): 80–7.

Weiss, Bernhard, and Jeremy Wanderer, eds. 2010. *Reading Brandom: On Making It Explicit*. London and New York: Routledge.

Wheeler, Samuel C. 2000. *Deconstruction as Analytic Philosophy*. Stanford: Stanford University Press.

Williams, William Carlos. 2000. *Selected Poems*. London: Penguin Books.

Williams, William Carlos. 2013. *Paterson*. Edited by Christopher John MacGowan. New York: New Directions Books.

Wittgenstein, Ludwig. 1966. *Lectures and Conversation on Aesthetics, Psychology and Religious Belief*. Edited by Cyril Barrett. Oxford: Blackwell.

Wittgenstein, Ludwig. 1974. *Philosophical Grammar*. Translated by Anthony Kenny. Oxford: Blackwell.

Wittgenstein, Ludwig. 1981. *Zettel*. Translated by Gertrude E. M Anscombe. Oxford: Blackwell.

Wittgenstein, Ludwig. 1997. *Denkbewegungen: Tagebücher 1930–1932, 1936–1937*. Innsburck: Haymon Verlag.

Wittgenstein, Ludwig. 1998. *Culture and Value*. Translated by Peter Winch. Oxford: Blackwell.

Wittgenstein, Ludwig. 2001a. *Remarks on the Foundations of Mathematics*. Edited by G. H. von Wright and Rush Rhees. Translated by G. E. M Anscombe. Oxford: Basil Blackwell.

Wittgenstein, Ludwig. 2001b. *Tractatus Logico-Philosophicus*. London and New York: Routledge.

Wittgenstein, Ludwig. 2008. *The Blue and Brown Books*. Oxford: Blackwell.

Wittgenstein, Ludwig. 2009. *Philosophical Investigations*. Translated by Gertrude Elizabeth Margaret Anscombe, Peter Michael Stephan Hacker, and Joachim Schulte. Malden, MA, Oxford and Chichester: Wiley-Blackwell.

Wittgenstein, Ludwig. 2013. *The Big Typescript*. Translated by C. Grant Luckhardt and Maximilian E. Aue. Malden, MA, Oxford and Chichester: Wiley-Blackwell.

Index

absolute
    absoluteness   128, 133
    'Absolute Spirit'   45, 123, 127
    knowledge   20–1, 120, 125
    literary   54, 92
    meaning   76
    nature   25, 58–60
    vs. perspectival   118, 123–4
    truth   5, 65, 75, 86–7, 91
action   23, 60–1, 65–6, 70
aesthetics
    analytic/continental   1, 73, 95–6
    etymological sense of   5–6, 121–2
    of the fragment   39–40, 118
    romantic   44
aeternae veritates   17, 20, 37, 120
agreement   9, 33, 89–91
analytic and continental
            philosophy   2, 44, 143
analytic-continental divide   1, 4, 11, 73, 77, 95, 142
analytic philosophy   1–4, 11–12, 29, 53, 57, 86
aphorism   39–40, 74, 118
Apollonian/Dionysian   97, 100, 102, 106
appearance-reality   16, 26, 48, 71, 99–100, 131–2
Aristotle   44, 81
art
    artforms   102, 107, 111, 115
    as perspective   19, 26, 115–17, 121, 128
    philosophy of   95–7, 134
    poetry   8, 43–4, 48, 82–4, 92, 111, 115, 130–5
    science   41, 77
    work of   31–2
aspect seeing   8, 110, 113, 115
Austin, John L.   5, 16, 61, 99

belief   6, 17–21, 60–1, 64–5, 85–7

Blackburn, Simon   24–5, 51–2, 59–60, 66–71, 91–2
Brandom, Robert   22–3, 51–8, 60–5, 69–71, 92

Cavell, Stanley   3, 96, 104–5, 112
child   76, 79, 112–13, 127–8, 134
Christianity   128–9, 133
common
    communication   18, 31, 41, 89–92, 108
    community   18, 20, 64, 84, 89–92
    essence   82–3
    language   18–19, 63–4, 88–9, 132
concepts   17–21, 33–8, 76, 80–4, 86, 89–90
conceptual scheme   90–2, 124
context
    as form of life   54, 85, 88, 91
    as perspective   125–6
    poetic   108–12, 133
    as situation   111–12, 116, 121–2
continental philosophy   1–4, 57, 142
craving for generality   18, 80–1
creation
    creativity   19, 32
    and destruction   131–3
    linguistic and poetic   21, 33, 44, 62, 102, 113, 135
    of perspectives   133–4, 140–3
culture   64, 83, 85, 87–9, 91, 102–3, 125

Derrida, Jacques   4
Descartes, René   17, 21–2, 30, 39, 85, 88
discourse   1, 25, 58–9, 64, 96
doctrine   87, 117–24

epistemology   17, 30, 117–24, 134
essence
    essentialism   8, 16, 89, 96
    of language   12, 16–21, 32–5, 46–7, 75–9, 82, 130–2

eternal recurrence 129, 142
expression 7, 13, 30–2, 39–42,
      100–2, 137–8
expression and representation 97,
      100–2, 104, 137
expressivism. *See* Romantic Expressivism;
      Pragmatic Expressivism; Poetic
      Expressivism

fact
   and fiction 66–8
   and interpretation 86, 117, 120–1
   normative 59
   and statement 10–11, 42, 77
   and value 20
family resemblance 81–4, 89, 96
fiction 13–14, 60–1, 66–8, 96, 110–12
Fish, Stanley 110–12, 116
force 19, 31, 65–6, 86, 102
form of life 54, 65, 83, 85, 88–92
Frege, Gottlob 12–15, 99

god 21, 85, 100, 102, 135

Hamann, Johann Georg 29–41
Hegel, Georg Wilhelm Friedrich 40, 45,
      53, 57, 137
Heidegger, Martin 4, 7, 44–8, 51–
      2, 62, 135
Heraclitus 85, 127–8
Herder, Johann Gottfried von 29–41, 47
history and genealogy 37, 76, 89
Humboldt, Alexander von 29–32, 37–9

imagination 27, 112–13, 134
interpretation
   criticism and poetry 105,
      107–8, 112–13
   magic language 35, 42–3, 64, 76
   perspectivism 86–8, 110–11, 115–34
   relativism 84
invention 16, 27, 110, 141–2

Kant, Immanuel 25, 35, 62, 71, 117
knowledge 19, 21, 54, 86, 119–25, 127

language
   clarification 14, 22, 79, 88
   seduction and charms 20–2, 86
   social practice 21, 33–5, 37, 89
   traps 21, 78, 88, 102
language-games
   definition 79–82
   information 11, 103–5
   multiplicity 27–8, 61–3, 67–8,
      88–92, 101, 106–8
   poetry 111–13
   rules 20, 27, 59
Lichtenberg, Christoph
      Georg 29, 32, 38–41
logic 4, 12, 16, 36, 46–8, 86, 90–1

Mauthner, Fritz 7, 75
meaning
   context-independent meaning 5, 76
   meaningless statements 6, 13–14,
      37, 76, 108
   ostensive 10–11, 80
   reference 6, 9, 13–14, 29, 33, 80, 97
   use 9, 33, 56–7, 76
metaphilosophy 38–9, 41
metaphor
   dance and laughter 137–8
   mirror and lamp 54–6
   origin of language 17–20, 34–5,
      83–6, 123–6, 132
   poetic language 15, 76, 105
metaphysics
   critique 32–9, 59–60, 66–71, 73–82,
      97–103, 128–35, 141
   end 30, 44–5, 74–6
   language and truth 5–7, 9–28, 47–9,
      85–8, 117–25, 139
method 78, 80, 91, 95, 128, 142
morality 83, 85, 128–9, 131, 133
music 100–7, 138

naturalism 60, 67
Nietzsche, Friedrich
   Beyond Good and Evil 19–22,
      39, 45, 64, 82–3, 85, 87, 122,
      125, 127, 139–40, 147 n.9,
      148 n.10, 150 n.6
   The Birth of Tragedy 100–2, 121,
      124, 128–9, 138
   Dawn 43, 147 n.9, 150 n.6
   Dionysus Dithyrambs 98,
      100, 154 n.1
   The Gay Science 19, 75, 116–17, 123,
      128–32, 138

Human, All Too Human   17, 19, 75,
     126, 138, 146 n.6
On the Genealogy of Morals   43,
     123, 148 n.10
*On Truth and Lie in a Nonmoral
     Sense*   17–18, 20–1, 35, 86, 102,
     123, 125–7
Thus Spoke Zarathustra   43, 99, 127,
     134, 137–8
Twilight of the Idols   11, 16, 40, 81,
     84–5, 100, 141, 157 n.1
The Wanderer and his Shadow   17,
     49, 76, 126, 147 n.6
Novalis   30, 40–4

objectivity   122, 125, 127, 129, 131
ordinary language. *See* uses of language
originality   19, 132

perception   5, 35–6, 121–5, 130
performative   74, 118, 122
perspectivism   5–8, 65–71, 86–8, 91–2,
     117–27, 130–4
philosophy of language
     ideal language philosophy   12,
          22, 56, 86
     ordinary language philosophy   12,
          15, 33–4, 56
     poetic philosophy of
          language   8, 96, 139
philosophy of the future   139–42
Plato
     Cratylus   9, 19, 33, 60
     poetry   1, 137
     Platonism   5, 16–17, 26–7, 45, 81,
          97–101, 131
pluralism   25, 61–3, 65–8, 91
poetic expressivism   7, 74, 95–6, 137
poetic language. *See* uses of language
poetics   5, 8, 44, 96–8, 117–18, 135, 138
poetry
     art   19, 77, 82, 84, 115–16,
          130, 134–5
     definition   96–7, 101–13,
          131, 137–41
     language   5, 30, 40–2, 46–8,
          73–4, 90–2, 103
     philosophy   1, 3–8, 11, 25–6, 43–4,
          47–8, 74, 95–6, 130, 134–5
     poiesis   26, 44, 76, 92, 130, 135, 137

practice   108, 111–12
rejection   1, 4, 61, 97–9, 137
truth   41, 90, 102
Ponge, Francis   109
pragmatic expressivism
     contrast to Romantic
          Expressivism   7, 32, 61–2,
          65, 68, 73
     definition   7, 51–4, 56–61, 69–71
     intersection with Romantic
          Expressivism   71, 92,
          95, 101, 137
pragmatism   22–30. 51–9, 69–
     71, 91–3, 120
Price, Huw   10–11, 51–2, 54–5, 58, 60,
     62–3, 66–70, 76, 92
psychology   85, 125

rationality   1, 51, 54, 71, 84–5, 91–2
reading-as   8, 97, 107–8, 115, 117
reason   5–6, 53–4, 60–4, 71,
     85, 91–2, 122
relativism   5–7, 59–60, 68–9, 75, 83–4,
     87, 90–2, 124
religion   83, 85, 128–30, 133, 135
representationalism
     conception of language and truth   4–
          8, 10–15, 65–8, 96–104, 137
     critique of   19–27, 58–60, 76–80
     epistemological
          framework   30–2, 119–22
rhetoric   118, 120
rhythm   107–9, 138
Rimbaud, Arthur   85
romantic expressivism
     contrast to Pragmatic
          Expressivism   7, 51–4, 61–2,
          65, 68, 73
     definition   7, 31–2, 47–9
     intersection with Pragmatic
          Expressivism   71, 92,
          95, 101, 137
romanticism   24, 27–8, 30, 51–2, 93
Rorty, Richard   11–12, 20–7, 59,
     63–4, 129–30
rules   20, 33, 59–60, 75, 84, 90,
     106–7, 112
Russell, Bertrand   12–15

Schlegel, Friedrich   40–4

Schleiermacher, Friedrich
    Daniel Ernst   35
science
    independence   45–8
    and language   17, 41, 83
    perspective   67, 77, 121, 124,
        128–30, 133–5
    propositions   14–15
    scientism   67, 70, 80, 128–9
seeing-as   107–13, 122, 125–6,
    132, 134–5
semantics   10–12, 22–3, 56–7, 103–4
sense
    making   77, 84, 88, 99, 102–3, 107–8,
        110–13, 116, 135
    Sinn   13–14, 48
    sound and   104
significance
    language   99, 113
    poetry   95, 97, 99, 105–6
situation. *See* context
sound   33–6, 90, 109
speech   35–7, 104, 110, 113
style   39–43, 64, 74, 137–8, 148
subjectivity   56, 123–4
system   40–2, 74, 90–1, 141–2

Taylor, Charles   30–2, 62, 74, 76
therapy   74, 78, 142–3
thing-in-itself   21, 25, 37, 125
transformation   74, 108, 127, 134
translation   35–6, 105, 126
truth
    absolute. *See* absolute
    correspondence   5–7, 10, 19–24,
        41–2, 119–21
    critique of absolute   86–7, 90–2, 127
    disclosure   5–7, 30–2, 76–8
    poetic   98–102, 141–2
    satisfaction of desires   65–9

    significance   77
truth-value   13–15

unconscious   125, 132–3
understanding   101–6, 111–12
uses of language
    ideal language   15, 78–9, 86
    metaphysical language   20–1, 33–5,
        75, 78, 85, 102, 125
    ordinary/everyday language   15–16,
        48, 78, 81, 88, 103–5, 110
    poetic/literary language   4, 8,
        26, 33, 47, 96, 102–10, 113,
        115, 137, 139

value   6, 20, 86–92, 117–19,
    124–7, 139–42
vocabulary   24–6, 56–7, 63–4

Williams, William Carlos   108–10
Wittgenstein, Ludwig
    The Blue and Brown Books   16, 80–1,
        89, 142, 145 n.1
    Culture and Value   87–8,
        113, 115, 138
    Lectures on Aesthetics   89, 107
    Philosophical Grammar   79, 105
    Philosophical Investigations   11, 15,
        22, 69, 79–82, 84–5, 88, 90, 101,
        104, 106, 111, 140, 142, 148 n.9
    *Philosophy of Psychology–A
        Fragment*   89, 107, 110–13, 122
    *Remarks on the Foundations of
        Mathematics*   105
    *Remarks on the Philosophy of
        Psychology, Volume 1*   107
    Tractatus Logic-Philosophicus   4, 6, 9,
        12, 14–16, 78–9, 145 n.1
    Zettel   11, 103
writing   37–42, 74, 118, 137–8

www.ingramcontent.com/pod-product-compliance
Lightning Source LLC
Chambersburg PA
CBHW061837300426
44115CB00013B/2430